Growing Pains in Ministry

Growing Pains in Ministry

Sean D. Sammon

AFFIRMATION BOOKS
WHITINSVILLE, MASSACHUSETTS

Income derived from the sale of Affirmation books is used by the House of Affirmation to provide care for priests and religious suffering from emotional unrest.

AFFIRMATION BOOKS is an important part of the ministry of the House of Affirmation, International Therapeutic Center for Clergy and Religious, founded by Sr. Anna Polcino, S.C.M.M., M.D.

Cover design by Rosemary Fay, S.N.D. deN.

Dedication

To my parents,
Mary Bradley Sammon
and
Matthew G. Sammon,
with thanks
for their love and companionship
on life's journey

Published with ecclesiastical permission

First Edition

© 1983 by House of Affirmation, Inc.

Library of Congress Cataloging in Publication Data

Sammon, Sean D., 1947–
    Growing pains in ministry.

    Includes bibliographical references.
    1. Pastoral theology—Catholic Church. 2. Catholic Church—Doctrinal and controversial works—Catholic authors. I. Title.
BX1913.S27 1983   262'.1   83-9991
ISBN 0-89571-016-1

Printed by
Mercantile Printing Company, Worcester, Massachusetts
United States of America

Contents

Foreword

There is but one *mission* in the Church as proclaimed by Jesus: to bring health and holiness to all of creation. The Second Vatican Council announced anew this mission of the Church: "that by spreading the kingdom of Christ everywhere for the glory of God the Father, she might bring all men [and women] to share in Christ's saving redemption; and that through them the whole world might in actual fact be brought into relationship with Him" (*Apostolicam Actuositatem*, 2). Jesus desires that every area of human life be touched by his saving grace. "The joys and the hopes, the griefs and the anxieties of the [people] of this age, especially those who are poor or in any way afflicted, these too are the joys and hopes, the griefs and anxieties of the followers of Christ. Indeed, nothing genuinely human fails to raise an echo in their hearts" (*Gaudium et Spes,* 1).

While it is accurate to state that there is but one mission of Christ's Church, it is also accurate to state that there are many ministries within that Church. Ministry flows from the one mission of the Church, but each ministry is unique. No one ministry is identical with the common mission.

Ministries should provoke a call to real spiritual leadership—a leadership to minister to people, to help them become more aware of their gifts and how they can serve the Kingdom.

Leadership is based on the fact that God has called us to do his work and has given us whatever we need to respond effectively. He has invited us to join in his style of personhood which

9

is life-affirming and life-creating. The apostles became aware of their potential in being called by Christ. He made the Samaritan woman aware of who she was, aware of her poverty, but also of her potential. Jesus invited her response to him. To call one another to life—this is one of the most basic tasks of ministry. It means to help one another discover the real meaning of life so that each one may become the unique creature God intended. Such a leadership demonstrates the ministry of healing, compassion, and forgiveness of the Father. At a point in time when so many people feel unaccepted and alienated from family, community, and country, it becomes a ministry that gives special witness to the presence of God's Kingdom here on earth.

In *Growing Pains in Ministry,* Brother Sean D. Sammon, F.M.S., Ph.D., a dedicated religious and distinguished clinical psychologist, invites us to renew our personal understanding of ministry. This wise and balanced book is a genuine guide to understanding adult development in ministry. At the library, we can find many books on child and adolescent psychology; only recently have a substantial number of books on adult psychology appeared. Adulthood is now seen to be far different from that plateau of stability we contemplated when we were teenagers. In our Christian tradition, adult "life cycle" is often referred to as "pilgrimage" or "faith journey." The road to full maturity leads through ever-changing terrain, periods of dormancy as well as spurts of growth.

Our society rewards those who achieve external success. Life in Christ's ministries, however, gives its most precious rewards to those who achieve internal success by completing the personal journey to emotional and spiritual maturity. The road to this integrity and maturity is a survival trip across unknown territory. Although every minister travels this road, few leave signposts and markers along the way. Fortunately, this book will serve as a traveling companion for our journey in ministry. *Growing Pains in Ministry* will challenge our thought and encourage our faith.

Commenting on Matthew 5:14, "You are the light of the world," John Paul II writes:

> It is disconcerting for us, aware as we are of our littleness and sinfulness, to hear addressed to us the clear words: "You are the light of the world." The Apostles must have trembled at hearing them. So have thousands of people since then. And yet the Lord spoke those words to people whom he knew to be human, limited and sinful. For he also knew that they were to be light not by their own strength but by reflecting and communicating his light, for he said of himself: "I am the light of the world" (Jn 8:12, 9:5; cf. 1:5, 9; 3:19, 12:46).[1]

Growing Pains in Ministry will bring those of us in ministry closer to an understanding and a comfortableness in being the light of Christ to others, even when we may tremble to do so.

I personally found this book most rewarding reading. Even though at times it seemed to increase my "growing pains," it encouraged me to love my ministry even more. I know by faith that this era is for us and for all who call upon the name of the Lord the age of the Church. The greatest gift God has given us is to live now and to call this age our own. Supported by faith in Jesus, affirmed by good books like this present work, we can be sure that the mission of the Church will be carried forward by the many ministries in which we are called to "witness unto Christ."

Thomas A. Kane, Ph.D., D.P.S.
Priest, Diocese of Worcester
Publisher, Affirmation Books
Whitinsville, Massachusetts

Feast of the Ascension
12 May 1983

---

1. L'Osservatore Romano, 9 March 1981, p. 17.

Preface

People of every era believe that their age is a special time in human history. When the analysts write the history of our present Church era, how will they judge it: as a watershed in the history of Christianity, or just a time of upheaval; as an age of faith, or one of unbelief; as a period of renewal, or a time of destruction? Whatever their conclusions, future chroniclers will need to admit that contemporary Roman Catholicism has within it all the makings of a revolution. A difficult time for many people, the events of the period have transformed a number of men and women into genuine believers. They could well be the people that the Spanish philosopher and writer Miguel de Unamuno described as believing in a real God and not just the idea of one. They have passion in their hearts, anguish in their minds, uncertainty, doubt, and an element of despair even in their consolation.

The "changes" that have come about in the Catholic Church as a result of the Second Vatican Council are nothing short of amazing. Affecting nearly every aspect of Church life, they destroyed a parochial and comfortable religious world view and redirected considerable religious energy into what was once known as the "secular" realm. Many existing signs, though, suggest that even fifty years hence, the hindsight of history will judge the recent disappearance of once familiar religious understandings and practices as only a clearing-away process leading to real renewal.

Church ministers, in particular, have felt the effects of a changed but as yet unreformed Church. Patrick Glynn, senior editor of the *Journal of Contemporary Studies,* observed recently that the period since Paul VI's encyclical on birth control has been marked by self-doubt and dissension within the Church. A number of statistics support his observation. For example, since 1966, 11,000 American priests and 35,000 women religious have resigned from their dioceses and congregations; weekly mass attendance has dropped precipitously; some clergy and lay Catholics have clashed bitterly with bishops on issues of contraception, abortion, divorce and remarriage, the ordination of women, and priestly celibacy.

Parallel to these developments has been an enormous growth in real interest about social justice concerns. Rooted in the spirit of documents such as Paul VI's *Populorum Progressio* (1967), John XXIII's *Mater et Magister* (1961) and *Pacem in Terris* (1963), and the Council's *Gaudium et Spes* (1965), the Church has placed new emphasis on peace and disarmament, and Third World concerns. Over the last ten years, for example, about 90 percent of the nation's Catholic religious orders and 60 percent of its 173 dioceses and archdioceses have established peace and justice commissions. Public stands have been taken on a variety of political issues: United States aid to El Salvador, housing policy and rent controls, and nuclear disarmament. Today's Church is not the parochial one of twenty years ago in which the political involvement of many official Church personnel would have been limited to matters such as federal aid to parochial schools and other areas where the interests of the Church were directly at stake.

What is really happening within Roman Catholicism? What is the meaning of the "growing pains" that the Church and its ministers are experiencing? Are the choirs, now bare and ruined, to remain that way? Has renewal run its course or is the first real chance for it only now at hand? How has the change and upheaval of the past twenty years affected Church ministers?

In a context other than Church renewal, social scientists recently developed an interest in psychological and emotional change and growth throughout the adult years. They report that most men and women mature through a series of alternating stable and transitional periods. During times of stability people set their sights on the future and feel they are building a life for themselves. In contrast, transitional periods are times for second thoughts. Sights are set on the past; one's personal life structure is reviewed.

Today's Church ministers live within a Church that is in transition. Their Church, religious orders and congregations, and the ordained priesthood are seeing the effects of transitional change. With this understanding, Church ministers go through their own times of personal stability and transition. For all involved, the present Church era is one of uncertainty and stress. In this book I will examine several aspects of the recent changes in Roman Catholicism and also the personal development of the sisters, priests, and brothers who are among its many ministers.

This book, then, is about change. It is divided into three parts. The first, "Making Sense of Change," examines transitions. These periods of change, upheaval, and chaos compel us to ask fundamental questions. In chapter one, I introduce the concept of transition and discuss its three characteristic features. Next, in chapter two, I apply our understanding about transitions to recent changes seen within the Church, religious orders and congregations, and the ordained priesthood. Chapter three concludes the first section and contains a discussion of recent developments in the American *social character* and uses these notions to enhance our understanding of transitions in Church life and religious leadership.

In part two, "Change and Adult Maturity," I examine the adult development of priests and men and women religious from the late teen years until the end of the life cycle. Chapters dealing with novice adulthood, midlife, and later adulthood and retirement document aspects of the personal, interpersonal, and spiritual journey that Church ministers make during their adult years. Specific issues such as second thoughts about life commitments, the growing awareness of mortality that occurs about midlife, intimate relationships, retirement, and the process of mourning are discussed in some detail.

Part three, "Celibacy, Spirituality, Fidelity, and Change," include chapters on several thorny issues that many Church ministers face. First, I discuss the evolution of celibacy over the course of the life cycle. Celibacy is examined as a charism and not as a discipline. Next, I consider the development of faith and spirituality during the adult years. Defining faith as our answer to the question, "On whom or what do I set my heart?" I examine people's responses at different way stations on the journey of belief. Permanent commitments are the subject of the penultimate chapter. Are they possible during an age of transition, and, if so, how do we justify these total and seemingly irrevocable promises? Finally, section three closes with a discussion of stress and burnout. The present age is also one of stress. Times of personal transition add to the discomfort many of us already feel. Is burnout, that sense of physical, psychological, and spiritual exhaustion, an inevitable part of ministry in today's Church? Can we identify the early warning signs of burnout and take steps to cope with them?

This book was written on the run, in several locations and at various times. Its contents have been presented at a number of workshops over the past five years. In that way, much of the material has been tested against the recent experience of Church ministers. It is meant to be a helpful and practical book, simple and straightforward, with ample footnotes and references for the reader who wishes more information on any of the topics presented briefly in these pages. I am thankful to the many men and women attending workshops and symposia sponsored by the House of Affirmation, and to many present and former residents of the House for their provocative and challenging questions about change in the Church and in themselves. Their efforts have helped make the notions in this book clearer and more relevant to the lives of Church ministers.

In writing a book I have learned many things, the first being that no book is written alone. I am thankful to several people who have helped this material see the light of day. Father Thomas A. Kane, Ph.D., D.P.S., and Sister Anna Polcino, S.C.M.M., M.D., have encouraged me to write, made helpful suggestions about the material, and were supportive with their interest as the book took shape. Several colleagues and friends read early drafts of various chapters and made a number of clarifying suggestions. If this book is easy to read, clear, and consistent, they need to receive the credit. They should not, however, be held responsible for its conclusions. Among them, I appreciate the efforts of Sister Nuala Harty, O.L.A., Brother Martin Helldorfer, F.S.C., John E. Kerrigan, Jr., Sister Marie Kraus, S.N.D., and Brother John P. Nash, F.M.S.

I have also learned that in writing a book, hope wanes at times, the task appears overwhelming, and the desire to abandon the project is great. Several friends got me over these hurdles, in particular, Craig F. Evans, Brother John Mulligan, F.M.S., and Brother Ronald D. Pasquariello, F.M.S. I am thankful also to Mrs. Terry Murphy and Mrs. Jacqueline Sullivan, who typed parts of the manuscript. Sister Marie Kraus, S.N.D., executive editor of Affirmation Books, deserves special mention. Her ability to suggest a clarifying phrase, a way to organize a chapter, or a point needing additional development made the writing of this book easier and eminently more enjoyable. I am thankful to her for the many hours of time and personal support that she contributed to this effort. The members of my religious congregation, the Marist Brothers of the Schools, also deserve mention for their support of my work over the past several years. Professional religious educators for the most part, they are an exceptional group of men. As a community we are in transition, searching for effective and appropriate ways to let people know that the news of the Lord Jesus is indeed good. Finally, I am thankful to my parents. Their lives have taught me a great deal about change, growth, and the life cycle. Watching them grow older with wisdom and integrity, I have hope in the future. It is to both of them that this book is dedicated.

Sean D. Sammon, F.M.S.
27 February 1983   Whitinsville, Massachusetts

Part I: Making Sense of Change

Chapter One

Life transitions

"Middle age is a wonderful country," John Updike tells us, "all the things you thought would never happen are happening." Elaborating on his observation, novelist Updike concedes that by midlife you are tired of being young—there is too much wasted energy to it. "For years nothing happens; then everything happens. Water boils; the cactus blooms; cancer declares itself."[1] Stated simply, around age forty one of life's transitions gets under way.[2]

Updike describes well the life transition that initiates middle age. This passage from early adulthood into the middle years, though, is but one of several periods of transformation occurring periodically in people's lives. Transitions are times of disorientation and reorientation that mark the turning points of the path of growth.[3] Webster points out that the word comes from

---

1. John Updike, *Rabbit is Rich* (New York: Ballantine Books, 1981), pp. 214, 366.

2. For more detailed studies of life transitions, see William Bridges, *Transitions* (Reading, Mass.: Addison-Wesley, 1980); Arnold Van Gennep, *The Rites of Passage,* trans. Monika B. Vizedom and Gabrielle L. Chaffee (Chicago: University of Chicago Press, 1960); and Naomi Golan, *Passing through Transitions: A Guide for Practitioners* (New York: Free Press, 1981).

3. Bridges, *Transitions,* p. 5.

the Latin *transitio* and means a passage from one stable place or stage of development to another.[4]

Everyone experiences transitions. These periods of self-renewal occur regularly during life. In the midst of one, some people feel backed into a corner and frustrated. Others feel scared, hopeless and confused, or lonely and alienated. A number of events can initiate a personal transition: inner promptings toward growth, arriving at a certain age, changing ministries, a new relationship, questions about life choices and commitments, or a serious illness, to name a few.

Once we understand transitional experiences we can examine the adult growth of Church ministers and make sense of the emotional, spiritual, and interpersonal changes they undergo.

In this chapter I will focus on transitional times, describing their characteristic features and discussing their place in the life cycle. To accomplish this task I will first briefly identify the three phases of any life transition and then examine generally the challenge of each phase. Finally, I will propose some guidelines for coping with times of personal transition.

The three phases of a transition

Psychologist Daniel Levinson describes life transitions as tremendous gifts and burdens.[5] These special lengthy times of change and growth have three characteristic aspects: an *ending*; a *period of darkness and exploration*; and finally, a *new beginning*.

Close examination reveals that every transition begins with an ending. A young married woman discovers that she is pregnant. This discovery brings joy but also a sense of loss as one phase of her life comes to a close. Another woman, leaving one job to take a more rewarding one, also experiences an ending. Her daily routine, schedule, and relationships with previous coworkers change. Though excited about her new position's novel and

---

4. See *Webster's New Collegiate Dictionary* (Springfield, Mass.: G. & C. Merriam, 1960).

5. Daniel Levinson et al., *The Seasons of a Man's Life* (New York: Alfred A. Knopf, 1978), p. 84.

attractive features, this woman also feels some fear, a sense of ending, and a loss of the familiar. Several reactions come with the transition's first phase: a sense of loss, grief for what must be surrendered, and fear that the future will not be so satisfying as the past.

Between the ending and the new beginning, there is an important period when people feel "up in the air," stranded, with few options for coping with their situation. This empty, fallow time between the ending and the new beginning is the core of any life transition and a difficult phase for most people. Men and women can usually endure being "up in the air" if it has meaning for them or moves them toward a desired end. However, when they cannot make much sense of the experience, distress results.

Every life transition ends with the beginning of a new phase in life. If you were asked to write your autobiography, think of those times you would write, "A new chapter of my life began when. . . ." Making this claim often signals the end of a life transition. For some people, new life chapters include a new self-image; for others, new projects and goals. Consider the middle-aged priest assigned to a new parish. How does he renew his enthusiasm for his life and work? In what way does he prepare for a new chapter of his life? He first mourns his old ministry and some of its relationships and involvements. Sharing his loss with others, he is better able to accept and cope with it. He also involves himself with his new congregation and takes care of himself in small ways. We would hope that eventually an optimistic state of mind is able to take root.

Mary Gordon, writing about contemporary Catholic working-class mores and manners, provides a graphic description of a transition's new beginning phase in her novel *Final Payments.* Isabel Moore had nursed her invalid father for eleven years. Now, she has a chance to create a new life for herself. Before taking up this challenge, however, she must make some final payments to her past and those who were part of it. Isabel attends to the ending and "up-in-the-air" phases of her transition during the course of the novel. As the book closes she takes her first shaky steps toward a new beginning. "I packed my things. I felt my own weakness, as if something hidden and growing had been taken from my body. I was light now, my body felt high again, and dexterous, and clever. But I was weak; I felt the delicious shakiness of an invalid in the first stages of his cure."[6]

In summary, life transitions are difficult times. One lets go of some old and familiar situations, people, and self-images. A period of darkness and confusion follows, and finally a new beginning. For many men and women the transition's new beginning phase is untidy but poses little difficulty. The ending and "up-in-the-air" phases, however, can be quite troublesome.

Endings

Endings are difficult and complex: they often leave us with unfinished business and lingering memories. Closing the cover on a novel, for example, you may find the characters lingering in your imagination; the book might have ended but the story is hardly over. Real life endings are similar. When moving, people usually spend some time saying good-bye to neighbors, sorting, discarding, and packing. They thus bring to a close a chapter of their life, but their story continues as they take with them memories of their neighbors, former home, and old neighborhood.

A mourning process is an important aspect of the first phase of most transitions. It begins during the first phase and continues well into the middle one. As with a loved one's death, the transitional person who mourns may experience grief and anger but also feelings of freedom and wonder.

Many endings are self-initiated. People decide to change jobs, begin or end relationships, or act on inner promptings toward growth. Occasionally, the actions of others trigger the transition's ending phase. A religious superior may encourage a sister, brother, or priest to change ministries. A lover ends a relationship suddenly. As one grows older, illness and death of contemporaries can trigger transitions.

Some endings begin with a clearing-away process. Recall the last time you changed residences. Remember all the items you

---

6. Mary Gordon, *Final Payments* (New York: Ballantine Books, 1978), p. 306.

gave away? And what about those once-prized "heirlooms" that found a new home on the junk heap? At any ending, people dismantle familiar structures. They break connections with familiar settings and finish with the past.

Endings are sometimes a two-edged sword. A young man leaves home to begin work or attend a college or seminary. Oftentimes, he experiences both relief and loneliness. This man's relief is part of his excitement about taking some steps toward independence. The loss of familiar relationships and his home's security, though, contribute to his loneliness.

Whether initiated by ourselves or others, most of us handle endings poorly. Terminations, losses, endings of any kind frighten us. This is due, in part, to our faulty understanding of them. Confusing endings with finality, we fail to see them as necessary first steps in a transitional process. Faced with an ending, rather than mourn our losses most of us want to avoid the whole experience. Elizabeth Kübler-Ross witnessed this avoidance again and again in her work with dying men and women.[7] Faced with death, life's most significant ending, many initially denied what was happening to them. Next, they became angry in another attempt to distance death. Time passed, bargaining failed, and a certain amount of mourning took place before these men and women finally accepted their imminent death. Like Kübler-Ross's patients, many of us think at first that any ending will be the end of us.

The first step of any transition includes the experience of "falling apart." Many people feel some loss and emptiness at this time. Their growth process can also look like a betrayal of their past. To arrive somewhere new, however, people first have to leave somewhere else.

Though parts of us will resist examining our coping style when faced with an ending, this knowledge is helpful. It can give us a better understanding of how we deal with any transition's first step. To begin with, childhood and family patterns influence our

---

7. See Elizabeth Kübler-Ross, *On Death and Dying* (New York: Macmillan, 1969) and *Death: The Final Stage of Growth* (Englewood Cliffs, N.J.: Prentice-Hall, 1975).

coping style in this situation. For example, were endings ignored? Was the change that came with them denied? A poignant illustration of this style occurred in a midwestern family whose seventeen-year-old boy, the oldest of six children, had been killed in a tragic farm accident. The boy's parents, brothers, and sister assembled at the wake. The mother and daughter, a wide-eyed seven-year-old, were sobbing quietly. The father and four boys, however, stood almost robotlike, appearing absent of any emotion. At one point, four-year-old Peter, the youngest boy, walked over, put his arms tightly around his father's leg, and began to weep. Almost immediately the child's father put his hand on the boy's head and whispered, "Peter, stop crying. I want you to be daddy's little man." Peter stopped weeping. He had learned this lesson: to deal with an ending and feelings of loss and sadness, one must engage in the parody of self-control and denial of feelings.

In other families, at any ending one member may experience anxiety and grief for the entire group. When moving from one neighborhood to another sometimes only one family member is visibly sad and upset. The others distract themselves quickly. They deny their feelings of loss or busy themselves with a host of activities and new relationships. Whatever our family's approach to endings, it has helped shape our own.

For a moment, examine your style of ending. Is it abrupt, designed to deny the impact of any change? If a parish priest, do you dash out of an assignment a few days before others expect your departure to avoid those "messy" good-byes? Or do you linger? Is your ending style slow and gradual? At a party does your host have to turn out the lights to give you the hint that everyone else left an hour ago? Some people's style is active in the face of an ending. A man with this style who retires as pastor would seek out others to say good-bye; participate in farewell parties in his honor; bring his work of leadership and a chapter of his life to a close. By facing his losses honestly he is also free to seek out new and age-appropriate ways to be of service to his Church. Other men and women let events happen to them because of their passive ending style.

Consider events that brought change into your life this past year. Were you fortunate enough to have a spiritual awakening, begin therapy, or fall in love? Did your appearance change as you gained weight or the results of your new exercise program became apparent? Perhaps your living situation became tense as new members joined the group. Did you leave active ministry? Become depressed? Lose a job or have a financial reversal? Perhaps you retired or a friend died suddenly. Maybe you began school or your family required more of your time and energies.

In considering recent changes in your life, select those most important for you. Recall how you dealt with the loss of your life circumstances and the person you were before the changes came. Was your reaction an active one? Or did you deny the impact of the changes? For example, even though it entailed some losses, did you insist that your promotion should give rise to a transition that was smooth and without stress? Author Alex Haley's remarks about his best-seller *Roots* capture some of the difficulty and distress that come with even "good events." Reflecting on the many losses and changes brought into his life by fame, Haley quipped, "I hope to God I never have anything like the *success* of *Roots* happen to me again."[8]

In sum, the challenge of the transition's first stage is clear: we need to let go of the person we used to be in order to find the person we are becoming in the new situation.

Darkness and Exploration

First there is an ending. Next we expect a new beginning. Instead, an uncomfortable fallow time falls in between. This middle phase of the transition is a most important one. One man compared its discomfort to stopping in the middle of a busy street to think. "Once you step off the curb," he said, "you need to get quickly to the other side. You'd have to be crazy to sit down in the middle of the street and figure things out."[9] Crazy or not, the transition's middle phase calls for us to stop

---

8. Jeffrey Elliot, "The Roots of Alex Haley's Writing Career," *Writer's Digest* (August 1980): 20.
9. Bridges, *Transitions,* pp. 112-13.

amidst life's business and take stock. We need to surrender to the confusion and emptiness that often accompany this work.

This crisis phase gives people a chance to review many things in their lives: commitments, beliefs, relationships, aspirations. Familiar problem-solving techniques generally do not work so well as in the past. During this "time-out" period men and women often suffer increased stress and are filled with doubts. Some find little meaning in their lives, wondering at times if life is worth living. Leo Tolstoy gives a powerful description of his experience with the transition's middle phase. "I felt," wrote Tolstoy, "that something had broken within me on which my life had always rested, that I had nothing to hold onto, and that morally my life had stopped."[10] Many religious professionals identify easily with Tolstoy's description. Consider the thirty-year-old religious sister who questions her life commitments. Grieving her loss of motherhood and current lack of intimacy, she wonders if she was mistaken in her earlier choice of life direction. Likewise, religious men at midlife can identify with a colleague's comments: "I seem to be asking the same questions at forty that I asked at eighteen. Who am I? Is this the life for me? Am I really close to anyone? If I were to die today what in my life would be left unlived? Should I make any changes?" No wonder people attempt to flee the struggle of the transition's middle phase.

During this phase men and women usually experience four unsettling feelings: disengagement, disenchantment, disidentification, and disorientation.

First, they feel disengaged and separate from a number of familiar places, persons, and events. As a consequence, they are better able to confront themselves and to see their relationships, God, values, aspirations, and life commitments in a new way. For example, in moving from his private life to public ministry, Jesus went into the desert. During those forty days, power, wealth, and prestige tempted him. In struggling with these forces

---

10. This quotation and an extended account of Tolstoy's crisis appear in his autobiographical work, *A Confession,* trans. Aylmer Maude (London: Oxford University Press, 1940).

he became deeply aware of several things: his God, himself, his future mission.

Second, people are frequently disenchanted during the transition's middle phase. Their world no longer feels real. The lesson of disenchantment begins with the discovery that to really change we must realize that some significant part of our old reality is in our head, not out there. The noble leader, the flawless parent, the perfect wife, the utterly trustworthy friend are an *inner* cast of characters.[11] Many common experiences can lead to disenchantment: a new ministry, serious failure, the death of one's parents, an outstanding achievement, and other personal and religious milestones. Most significant transitions, then, not only involve disenchantment in their middle phase, they begin with it.

Men and women can use their disenchantment to change and grow. Some surrender to it. This positive approach to disenchantment helps them mourn the loss of illusions about self, other people, and the way the world works. This mourning process takes time. It is important to remember, though, that life does not end because people become disenchanted. Rather, this experience can transform a man or woman. Those who refuse this challenge, however, become disillusioned. The action of their lives comes to a stop; their future growth is hindered. Instead of seizing an opportunity to mature, these people repeat their past mistakes with new actors.

Third, people lose their familiar roles and understandings of themselves. To describe this disidentification experience, Erik Erikson once used the wry wisdom of a sign over a western town's bar. "I ain't what I ought to be," it read, "and I ain't what I'm going to be. But I ain't what I was."[12]

Finally, middle-phase transitional men and women generally feel disoriented, confused, lost in an unfamiliar world. Things once considered important no longer seem to matter much. This experience of disorientation is certainly not enjoyable but can be meaningful. Despite its discomfort, all of us need to experience

---

11. Bridges, *Transitions,* pp. 98-102.

12. Ibid., p. 98.

transitional disorientation for one chief reason: we have to become lost enough to find ourselves.

The film *On Golden Pond* illustrates clearly the four unsettling feelings of the transition's middle phase. Norman Thayer, Jr., portrayed by Henry Fonda, is growing old and having difficulty doing so. Norman is "in his late seventies"; his wife, Ethel, is "in her late sixties"—both "just barely so." The film's action centers around Norman's eightieth birthday celebration. Forgetful and lacking energy, he also has unfinished business in his relationship with his daughter. All these circumstances work together to undermine the man Norman used to be. He feels lost and in the film actually loses his way on a once familiar path. His old and comfortable roles are gone also. No longer employed, Norman scans the want ads. Rather sarcastically, he suggests to Ethel his intentions to follow up on some of the job openings. Having shed his old roles, Norman feels useless and vulnerable, cut off from others and his former life. Finally, he feels disenchanted. What he once thought important and sought after has now lost its gleam and allure. During the course of the film Norman struggles to become someone who is at first unfamiliar to him.

Billy, a thirteen-year-old house guest, helps Norman move through his transition. Forgetting to screen the blaze he lit in the fireplace, Norman almost sets fire to the house. Billy comments about the resulting mess. In response, Norman barks at him, "I guess I'm just not safe to have around anymore." In a poignant scene, Ethel attempts to help Billy understand Norman's struggle. She counsels, "Sometimes you have to look hard at a man and realize that he's doing the best he can. He's just trying to find his way." During the middle phase of any life transition that is precisely what people are attempting to do: find their way. To accomplish their task, they need a large supply of patience and compassion.

The transition's middle phase, then, offers the possibility of transformation. People can enhance their ability to see and understand themselves and their world differently. There are many ways to accomplish this task. Finding time to be alone is important. Almost instinctively some men and women find ways to place themselves at a distance from familiar distractions. One man, for example, experiments with a directed retreat. Another vacations alone for the first time. Similarly, a middle-aged religious sister confides her increasing desire to steal off by herself. Rather than spend time with community members, she learns to enjoy her own company. During the transition's middle phase, there will be many new impulses and changes in people's lives. They need to learn not to feel guilty about them. Put simply, the transformation central to this phase of the transition is one of death and resurrection. This process is often romanticized when people are far from it, but the man or woman in the midst of dying and rising knows its challenge only too well.

Finding meaning in the transition's middle phase.

Confronted with the challenge of any life transition, many people feel overwhelmed. Is it possible, they wonder, to manage a transition gracefully and creatively? Or must they resign themselves to just muddling through? Although no transition is easy, a few guidelines may provide some shelter in a transitional storm.[13]

First of all, in facing a transition's empty in-between time, do not treat yourself like an appliance sent back to the manufacturer for adjustment. Human growth is a messy experience. It is not the adjustment of a few screws nor the replacement of some wires. Try to see development as an unfolding, a ripening. Look at the transition's middle phase as though it were a New England winter. Sometimes we may wonder if it will ever end; we find ourselves skidding on the ice much too often; we fantasize about faraway sunny resorts; but we also realize how necessary that winter is for the amazing spring that will follow.

Second, take your time during any transition. This directive cannot be emphasized enough. Any transition takes time. For transitions that occur periodically during one's adult life, the

---

13. For a more extended discussion of finding meaning in change see ibid., pp. 78-82.

necessary developmental work generally takes four to five years. Consider the woman who spent her twenties and thirties rearing children and making a home. Psychologists tell us that many such women experience an "empty nest syndrome" when they approach their early forties. They question their life's meaning now that the kids have moved out. Finding a suitable answer will take many women a lengthy period of time. Their developmental work will not be completed in a few days, weeks, or even months. So if you are faced with major or even minor transitions, remember: take your time.

Third, during a transition do not act just for the sake of action. Change can sometimes be merely an attempt to avoid the pain of the transition. People credit their discomfort to present living situations, ministry, other people—almost anything except themselves and their own transition. Worse yet, seeing the difficulty as being outside themselves, many people change these externals—again almost anything but themselves. All these factors may contribute to one's discomfort. However, attempting a "geographical cure" without also changing oneself will do little to assist in managing a transition.

Fourth, in the midst of life changes recognize why you are uncomfortable. Transitions have a characteristic shape: things end, there is a fertile emptiness, and then things begin anew. While doing transitional work, it is normal and necessary to feel disoriented, detached, without a role, and disenchanted. Rather than struggling to escape the emptiness, surrender to it. Understanding the transition's characteristic shape and feelings may not eliminate the discomfort, but this knowledge can reassure us that we are not going crazy.

Fifth, during any transition we are pushed, pulled, squeezed, and stretched. So, we need to take care of ourselves in small ways. One man may join a health club and find he feels better physically in spite of his internal turmoil. Scheduling days by the ocean, another person nurtures her love for the sea. She returns from these times refreshed and more at peace with herself. Taking care of oneself is not selfish. Rather, it demonstrates a healthy self-respect and assists one in coping with any transition.

Sixth, find someone with whom you can talk: a good friend, spiritual director, religious superior, community member, spouse, or professional counselor. We all need someone who will keep us honest. Sharing ourselves with another person also reduces the loneliness and isolation that are part of any life transition.

Finally, explore the other side of change to discover what is waiting in the wings of your life. Keeping a journal can help in this regard. One middle-aged woman religious, for example, used Ira Progoff's intensive journal technique and dialogued with previously unknown aspects of herself.[14] She discovered what she really wanted in life, what was important to her. In coming to know her talents and blind spots, this woman was better able to plan for her future.

New beginnings

New beginnings are available to everyone. Some of us, though, have difficulty with them and fear that real change will destroy our old ways of establishing security. It generally does. The English novelist John Galsworthy was surely right when he wrote, "The beginnings of all human undertakings are untidy."[15] Often indirect and unimpressive, genuine beginnings depend upon an inner realignment of deep longings, values, and motivations. Even when external opportunities bring them to our attention, new beginnings start within us. New life springs from the barrenness of the transition's middle phase; new forms emerge from it.[16]

When people are ready to make a new beginning, they will do so. Sometimes inner signals, ideas, impressions, or vague images point the way to their future. A woman religious, for example, seeks a change in ministry. She searches out options and assesses

---

14. For a detailed presentation of Progoff's intensive journal technique, see Ira Progoff, *At a Journal Workshop* (New York: Dialogue House, 1975).

15. John Galsworthy, *Over the River* (London: William Heineman, 1933), p. 4.

16. See Bridges, *Transitions,* pp. 134-50.

her talents and the needs of her Church and community. Getting no hint of a new direction, this woman becomes discouraged. Surrendering to the emptiness and quietness of her transition's middle stage, she eventually picks up subtle signals. The comments of a friend, the offer of an unexpected opportunity, and inner promptings move her toward a new and rewarding beginning in ministry.

In making any new beginning, we need to keep several points in mind. First of all, when the time is right for change, stop getting ready and act. Preparing for a new chapter in life can turn out to be an endless task. Like the person in therapy who collects insights but has little interest in behavioral change, some people put off making their new beginning. When the right time comes, stop getting ready to do it—and do it!

Next, we need to identify ourselves with the final results of our new beginning. Be it moving residences, ending a relationship, providing more time for ourselves, changing behavior, or beginning a new phase of life, we should think of ourselves as moving in that direction.

Finally, in any important new beginning, a preoccupation with immediate results can be damaging. Concentrate on the process of reaching your goal rather than on the goal itself. It is unrealistic to expect yourself to make a new beginning like a sprinter coming away from the starting line. Try not to become so invested in results that your efforts to achieve them get overlooked.

Conclusion

There is a bittersweet quality to most transitions. The Gospel of John illustrates that a seed must fall into the ground and die before new life can spring forth. However, when faced with death or the trauma of transition, most people are overwhelmed initially. Nevertheless, only by surrendering their familiar self-images and perceptions of the world can men and women experience the growth that the transition brings.

Former television news reporter Betty Rollin makes this point dramatically in *First You Cry*,[17] an intimate account of her

17. Betty Rollin, *First You Cry* (New York: Harper and Row, 1980).

struggle with breast cancer. When told that the lump in her breast was malignant, Rollin was shocked. During the months following this discovery everything appeared uncertain. In her book's epilogue, written five years after her mastectomy, the author documents her transitional journey.

She begins by speculating about life and death scares. For about six months after surviving a scare, people feel shaken and grateful. Their perspective on life changes. When the six months are up, however, this new perspective fades. "Business as usual" resumes. No longer afraid, people regain their feelings of invulnerability.

With cancer it is different. One is left a little bit afraid for the rest of one's life. The fear of death, however, did wonders for the quality of Rollin's life. It initiated significant changes and long-lasting transitional growth. She found, for example, that in being afraid of death she was less afraid of other things: bosses, her spouse, plumbers, rape, bankruptcy, failure, not being liked, the flu, aging. She worried less about people's opinion of her and thought more about where she was at the moment, what she was doing, and whether or not she liked it. Cancer made her less sensible, killed her guilt, and improved her taste in men.

These changed perspectives exacted a price. Shortly after losing her breast, Rollin was distressed about being unable to keep a strapless dress up. Today she feels fortunate: losing her breast saved her life. Unlike her friends past forty who shudder on their birthdays, Rollin feels further from death each year.

Many factors played a role in Rollin's transition: surgery, radiation, her reaction, and the reaction of friends and co-workers. They helped her let go of past understandings of herself and the world. Rollin captures her transition's paradoxical quality, though, when discussing the possibility of her cancer recurring. If it does she will not be a "good sport" about it—especially if her life is cut short. But even should that happen she predicts she will look back on the years since her surgery and know that she fully enjoyed them. "I will be forced to admit that the disease that is ending my life is the very thing that made it so good." Other life transitions are as bittersweet. They are times of pain and confusion that invite us to grow and develop. The very change that at first appears to be the "end of us" will, if embraced, enrich our life.

Transitions, then, are times of self-renewal that are filled with change, upheaval, and growth. Their characteristic shape includes an ending, an uncomfortable but ultimately productive middle phase, and finally a new beginning. Although many men and women shrink from them, transitions offer the possibility of transformation.

It is also important to remember, though, that every transition is a way station on the journey of life. Each is meant to be a temporary state, a place to visit but not to live forever. Psychologically, transitions bring us back home to ourselves and involve the integration of a new self-understanding with elements of our old one. Eleanor Roosevelt described well how the struggle and confusion of these times of transformation help us to become more truly ourselves: "Somewhere along the line of development we discover what we really are, and then we make our real decision for which we are responsible. Make that decision primarily for yourself because you can never really live anyone else's life."[18]

Today's religious professionals, however, are facing even greater challenges than dealing with personal transitions. Their country, Church, dioceses, and religious orders and congregations are also involved in major transitions. In the next chapter, I will examine transitions in the Church, priesthood, and religious orders and congregations, and in Chapter Three will focus on current changes in American society that influence our lives. In order to consider particular developmental challenges faced during our adult years, it is necessary to first gain an adequate understanding of how our lives fit within the context of these other phenomena.

---

18. Joseph P. Lash, *Eleanor and Franklin* (New York: W. W. Norton, 1971), p. 238.

Chapter Two

"That superbly destructive Council"

Departing from Eden, Eve attempted to minimize her loss. "Adam," she said, "look at it this way: we are entering into a period of transition." Adam was not amused. Many of today's religious professionals, like Adam, find little consolation in Eve's quip. They fear religious and priestly life is falling apart and, for a number of reasons, their concern is well-founded.

Causes for concern among religious and clergy

Three general areas trouble many people in priesthood and religious life: their aging and declining membership, the challenges of a psychological age, and questions about the psychological health and development of priests, sisters, and brothers.

To begin with, the median age of sisters, brothers, and priests continues to rise rapidly, currently fifty-two for priests in the United States.[1] At the same time, diocesan presbyterates and religious orders and congregations report fewer members as resignations, retirement, and death reduce their numbers. During Paul VI's pontificate (1963-1978), for example, 30,000 priests

---

1. See Auxiliary Bishop Nicolas Walsh's remarks before the United States bishops' meeting, November 18, 1982. Reprinted under the title "The Challenge of the Vocations Statistics," *Origins* 12, no. 27 (December 16, 1982): 425-27.

were laicized.[2] From 1966 through 1978, the American priesthood shrank in size by 10,000 members.[3] Religious brotherhoods reported 33 percent fewer men in 1978 than 1967, their peak membership year.[4] During the same period, the number of religious sisters in the United States declined by almost 30 percent.[5] In a 1975 report, the National Sisters' Vocation Conference suggested reasons for these losses: community pressures and life-style, an inability to be oneself within the community, a wish to marry, and a desire for human intimacy.[6]

Other factors have eroded religious and priestly life's membership. For example, the number of men and women entering novitiates and seminaries today is much smaller than in the mid-1960s. In the United States alone, from 1966 to 1978 the number of seminarians declined by 25,000.[7] At the present time, there are only 4,000 students for the priesthood in American theologates.[8]

Future membership projections are as grim. In 1981 the University of Chicago's National Opinion Research Center projected that by the year 2000 there will be about 25,000 active Roman Catholic priests, half of today's number.[9] Recently, *The Boston Globe* reported that if present trends in the Boston archdiocese continue, by the turn of the century there will be only 400 priests available to service Greater Boston's 425 parishes.

2. William J. Bausch, *Traditions, Tensions, Transitions in Ministry* (Mystic, Conn.: Twenty-third Publications, 1982), p. 12.

3. Ibid, p. 67.

4. Lawrence Cada et al., *Shaping the Coming Age of Religious Life* (New York: Seabury Press, 1979), p. 48.

5. Ibid.

6. National Sisters' Vocation Conference, *Women Who Have Left Religious Communities in the United States: A Study in Role Stress, Phase I* (Chicago: National Sisters' Vocation Conference, 1975).

7. Bausch, *Traditions,* p. 67.

8. Walsh, "Challenge of the Vocations Statistics," p. 427.

9. National Opinion Research Center and Center for Applied Research on the Apostolate; see R. A. Schoenherr's "Decline and Change," University of Wisconsin, 1981.

The facts behind these statistics are making their impact. Parishes are being established with little hope of ever having a resident priest: others are being consolidated or closed.[10] Religious orders and congregations are withdrawing from hospitals and closing schools. Religious professionals suffer from frustration, stress, and burnout. Requests for early retirement are mounting.

In the face of these developments, secular culture confronts brothers, sisters, and priests with new and disturbing challenges. The sexual revolution, for example, takes exception to traditional understandings of celibacy and chastity. Psychology is asking bold questions, such as what really motivates a commitment to religious or priestly life? For some men and women, this commitment reflects deep and important aspects of their personality and life with God. Others, however, choose religious and priestly life for more pragmatic reasons: to satisfy the need for a safe and secure life; to cope with sexuality; to provide an outlet for the need to serve.[11] Still others rely on their congregation or diocese for a sense of identity and purpose in life.

A number of religious professionals also wonder about their psychological health and development. Here again, social scientists fail to reassure them. For example, psychologist Eugene Kennedy and his colleagues at Chicago's Loyola University conducted a major study of American priests.[12] They found the majority of their nationwide sample to be "psychologically underdeveloped." The lives of these men were shaped by the expectations of others rather than by self-discovery. Status and security, not interest and ability, had prompted their vocational choice. Their personal identity was lost in their priestly role. They had colleagues and acquaintances but few intimate friends. Failing to understand their emotional life, they dealt with their feelings

---

10. Walsh, "Challenge of the Vocations Statistics," p. 427.

11. D. J. Sweeney, "Social Character of a Religious Order" (Ph.D. diss., Catholic University of America, 1974).

12. Eugene C. Kennedy et al., "Clinical Assessment of a Profession: Roman Catholic Clergymen," *Journal of Clinical Psychology* 33, no. 1 (1977): 120-28.

through intellectualization and repression. Their attitude toward authority and law was adolescent; they needed and resented both. Although these men were generally successful in their work and external adjustment, they were not fulfilled as persons.

In sum, people in religious and priestly life are fewer and older. Questions exist about the psychological health and development of a number of religious professionals. In the face of this evidence, do we mislead ourselves with talk of a new age dawning for Church ministers? Would our energies be better spent in adjusting to the possibility that religious and priestly life, once considered immutable, is today shifting, crumbling, and dying?

There are no simple answers to these important and sobering questions. We can easily delude ourselves by insisting that religious and priestly life's renewal calls for little more than the rearrangement of a few externals. However, it may be just as misleading to insist that these committed life-styles are in their final days. Sister Joan Chittister gives us some good and bad news about our present dilemma.[13] First, the bad news. The worst is not yet over for priesthood and religious life. The good news? A transition in both life-styles is at hand. Possibly galvanizing for us all, it will make a number of people uneasy. Why? Church people will begin to realize that their transition may not be so predictable, rapid, or painless as they had expected.

Our present transition

Our present transition differs from a number of previous ones. In the first place, it was not planned carefully and then put into practice. Instead, this transition witnesses to the hidden instincts of the Spirit and grace. For some people, this turn of events has brought an unforeseen consequence. Their response to the Church's transformation may be like the reaction of first-century Jewish leaders to Jesus. He was not the conquering king many had expected; his appearance and reign failed to support their dreams of an earthly kingdom. Unable to relinquish their

13. Joan Chittister, "The Future of Religious Life," *New Catholic World* 226, no. 1349 (September/October 1982): pp. 200-203.

notions of the Messianic Age, many of these leaders went elsewhere to find their deliverance. The People of God, especially a
number of religious professionals, run this same risk today.

Answering three questions will give us some understanding of
the present transition of religious and priestly life. To begin
with, is the Church itself in the midst of a transition? Next, what
are the phases in the life cycle of any religious order or congregation? Finally, what has the previous evolution of priesthood and
religious life been like?

A Church in transition

The Chinese have been given credit for an ancient curse: May
you live in a time of transition! Today's Church may be cursed;
without doubt it is caught up in a transitional time of change,
upheaval, and chaos.[14] Theologian Karl Rahner observes that
the Roman Catholic Church is in the midst of a revolution that is
unlike any preceding it with one exception: the early Church
community's decision to admit Gentiles without requiring prior
conversion to Judaism.[15] This decision introduced a radically
new period into Church history, for the Good News would no
longer be Jewish Christianity's export to the Diaspora. Instead,
still rooted in the historical Jesus, it would grow now on the soil
of paganism.

Today's People of God face a similar transition as they begin
a new age. To understand their present situation we need to examine that first revolution's effect on the Church.

---

14. For more detailed information on our present Church transition,
see Karl Rahner's "Toward a Fundamental Theological Interpretation
of Vatican II," *Theological Studies* 40, no. 4 (December 1979); and his
"Planning the Church of the Future," *Theology Digest* 30, no. 1
(Spring 1982).

15. Rahner, "Toward a Fundamental Theological Interpretation of
Vatican II."

The Church's three great theological epochs

Church history comprises three great theological epochs. Each one has presented an essential and basically different situation for Christianity.

Jewish Christianity

The first epoch was the short period of Jewish Christianity. It was dominated by the death and resurrection of Jesus and was visible from Jesus' time until about 60 A.D. Jerusalem was the Church's center.

Western European Christianity

The Apostle Paul initiated the second epoch when he declared circumcision superfluous for non-Jews. With this promulgation, Christianity began its movement from Jewish to gentile form. Many changes occurred: the Sabbath was abolished, the Church's center moved to Rome. Moral doctrines were modified; new canonical writings appeared and were accepted. During this first transition, Paul and the early Church community struggled with a major thelogical decision: what needed to be preserved of Jewish Law, Old Testament salvation history, and the Church of Jewish Christianity?

During the second great epoch, approximately 60 A.D. through 1960 A.D., Christianity became something of a western European "export." Roman-Hellenist culture influenced its form as did Europe's sixteenth-century colonialism and imperialism. Latin, for example, was exported to countries where it had never been an historical reality. Roman law was promulgated via canon law. The religious experience of other cultures was rejected and Western morality in all its details was imposed on the then known world. For example, in Africa, western-European Christianity replaced ancestral faiths and concepts, even terming African languages mere "dialects"; in Asia Christianity took little account of the great preexisting religions, such as Hinduism, Taoism, and Islam. These decisions, in part, explain Christianity's failure to take root in the Islamic world and some Eastern cultures.

Today's worldwide Church

Today the Church is entering its third great theological epoch. While never denying its historical roots, it is becoming truly a world Church. As a consequence, it recognizes its duty to enculturate Christianity into divergent societies. More native bishops, clergy, and religious are ministering in developing nations. The principle of autonomous regional churches is gaining acceptance, and different theologies are emerging to serve varied cultures. During this transition the Church community faces a challenge: how can unity be realized concretely within a pluralism of local churches? In answering this question, contemporary Christians must be as bold and as open as Paul. When did the present epoch really begin? What set it in motion? Can we identify its characteristic features as well as its successes and disappointments?

"That superbly destructive Council"

Our present theological epoch began just prior to the Second Vatican Council. A Counter-Reformation Church processed into Saint Peter's to begin that historic meeting; one much less certain in its form emerged. Rosemary Haughton refers to Vatican II as "that superbly destructive Council."[16] In so doing, she captures the transitional spirit that manifested itself between the Council's opening and closing ceremonies.

Trent had structured the era of post-Reformation Catholicism; Vatican I had reinforced it; now Vatican II ended it. The results of the termination can be seen everywhere. In the past twenty years the liturgy has changed more than during the previous dozen centuries. The ecumenical movement has reversed some of the effects of four hundred years of foot dragging and suspicion. The Church and many religious orders and congregations have taken serious steps to change their structures and customs. Understandings of authority have been transformed. Some decentralization has been implemented and collegiality fostered. The Council's documents gave fresh insight into the

16. Cited in Robert Imbelli's "Vatican II: Twenty Years Later," *Commonweal* (October 8, 1982): 522-26.

Church's nature and life. In *Pastoral Constitution on the Church in the Modern World* the entire Church took some responsibility for the world's future. The *Declaration on the Relationship of the Church to Non-Christian Religions* initiated for the first time in the Church's doctrinal history a truly positive evaluation of the great world religions.

Vatican II's fundamental meaning

Although these changes are the most obvious, Vatican II fulfilled a more fundamental role. It challenged the Catholic Church to make a really new beginning: to become a world Church. Such a challenge calls for a theological break in Church history. None like it has been seen since Paul the Apostle's time.

The wide-ranging implications of such a break are not apparent at first. Many things will have to change. To begin with, personal and institutional conversion needs to take place among Catholics. This transformation calls for openness to the Spirit, a life centered in the teachings of Jesus, and some fundamental changes in life-style oriented toward justice and a sharing of the world's goods.

Second, a world Church cannot be governed with the Roman centrism of recent Church history.

Third, the Good News will probably be proclaimed in many different ways, some we cannot imagine currently. If Christianity is to spread in new ways in Asia, Africa, the Islamic world, and even South and Central America, Church people need to return to the gospel's fundamental meaning.

Fourth, significant pluralism may exist among local churches, evident in such areas as canon law and liturgy. Consider what this might mean in terms of canon law: a Christian Massai chieftain in East Africa could live in the marital style of the patriarch Abraham. True liturgical pluralism needs to embrace much more than the use of different vernaculars.

Finally, in accepting world responsibility for freedom and justice, the Church undertakes to be courageous in meeting demands for social change, peace, and disarmament with concrete proposals. If, on the contrary, Christianity remains simply western European, as it was during the second of the Church's great theological epochs, it will have betrayed the fundamental meaning of Vatican II.

Disappointment with superficial changes

Many today are disappointed with the superficial adjustments effected so far by the Council. Many local liturgies continue to be only translations of the Roman liturgy. The recently promulgated new code of canon law may once again be a Western code imposed upon a world Church in Latin and South America, Asia, and Africa. Some fear it disregards the specific cultural contexts of many ethical questions. Expressing his exasperation with this situation, one South American bishop complained, "Why go on emptily intoning the glory of marriage in a land where most children are born out of wedlock?" Christians are reluctant to assume the task of social criticism. Finally, in some areas there is a widening gap between official Church teaching and what many of the faithful believe.

The transition's first phase

These viewpoints notwithstanding, there is another way to view the present Church situation—as the first stage of a transition.

The Church's present situation is a serious one. Today, some judge this institution to be more irrelevant than before the Council, a huge awkward giant unable to get into step with the march of history. Others fear it has lost its identity and sense of unity. Sociologist William McSweeney recently delivered a Council postmortem when he concluded that contemporary Roman Catholicism's search for relevance has led to the dead end of irrelevance. In his view *aggiornamento* has degenerated into accommodation, and theological pluralism merely camouflages the promiscuity of contemporary belief and practice.[17]

---

17. William McSweeney, *Roman Catholicism: The Search for Relevance* (Oxford: Basil Blackwell, 1980).

So, we ask, did something go wrong with renewal? What happened to the great optimism that accompanied the Council meeting? Is hope about the Church's future justified? Easy answers to these questions abound, but substantive ones are harder to find. Having lost their early optimism, some Catholics complain that Church leaders are interested in only cosmetic changes. Others see renewal not as a process but as a series of programs. Still others reduce the problem of renewal's apparent failure to a simplistic "too little coming too late." From the vantage point of his hermitage, for example, one wise and venerable Camoldolese monk concluded that the updating espoused by the Council was some seven centuries late.

Like personal periods of change, transitional times within a church have three characteristic aspects: breakdown and conflict; darkness and exploration; reintegration and new foundation.[18]

During the past two decades, the Catholic Church changed in a special way: it began to surrender its western European form. As might be expected during any transition's first phase, the Church experienced conflict and a sense of disintegration. The majority of Catholics, however, had not anticipated such results. As a consequence, like the British people during the early days of World War II, they have experienced many dark moments. However, they too can take hope from the words of Winston Churchill at that time: "This is not the end," said Churchill, "nor even the beginning of the end. It is, rather, the end of the beginning." The disintegration of the western European form of the Church is under way. Some of its familiar structures are already gone. This dying is the first stage of the Church's present transition; its real work of renewal can now begin.

---

18. This model has been suggested by Cada et al. in their analysis of transitions in religious life. It has been adapted here to be applicable to Church transitions. For further discussion of the model see Cada, *Shaping the Coming Age.*

Early signs of the transition's second phase

Today, some segments of the Church are moving into the transition's second phase, exploration and darkness. Men and women are searching out new gospel understandings and ways of being Christian. One reflection of this is *Newsweek's* recent observation that the world's Roman Catholic bishops appear to have set themselves up as a new branch of government.[19] National hierarchies are issuing moral report cards on their governments' programs. The United States bishops, for example, flatly rejected Reagan administration policies on nuclear deterrence. A document on capitalism and Catholic doctrine is being prepared for their 1983 discussions. In a seven-page analysis entitled *Ethical Reflections on the Economic Crisis,* Canada's hierarchy characterized their government's economic policies as immoral Social Darwinism. Specifically, the bishops stated, "The goals of serving the human needs of all people in our society must take precedence over the maximization of profit and wealth."

By their criticism of economic and political systems as unjust, a number of national hierarchies are becoming "otherworldly" in an unexpected way. Their countercultural positions, however, are consistent with past and present papal statements and give Church members hope for the future. Manila's Cardinal Jaime Sin summarized the situation's irony: "The moment the Church marries the system, the Church becomes the widow to the next generation."

The women's ordination movement is another example of the search for new forms in the Church. Also, the need for meaningful lay involvement at all levels within the Church has become apparent. Some members struggle to educate society about human rights issues. Finally, within the Church movements are under way addressing other important issues: women's liberation, poverty, sexual minorities, changing family structures, and biomedical and business ethics, to name a few.

Moving into this phase of exploration and darkness, Church members would do well to remember a few important points.

19. Kenneth Woodward and Anne Gregon, "Rendering unto Caesar," *Newsweek* (January 17, 1983): 51.

Any process of search and exploration brings tension, and members must be willing to live with it for at least several years.

Second, Christians will make more mistakes during this period than they will realize successes. Unless they enter into the transition's second phase expecting some failures, their process of search and exploration will lack creativity. Indeed, they can learn valuable lessons from their mistakes.

Finally, the search and exploration period will give rise to considerable diversity and pluralism within the Church. Members must be able to live with a certain amount of ambiguity. The work of the transition's second phase is a dying and rising that leads to purification. Eventually the painful process will give the Church greater vitality.

Religious professionals and the transition

Religious professionals did not escape the effects of this Church transition. Entering the period optimistically, many dioceses and religious communities made serious efforts to change their structures and customs. They reworked forms of government and modified styles of life and dress. Religious professionals hoped that these adaptations would bring about a surge of renewal, but their expectations were short-lived. Change proved to be slow, often leading to confusion and failure. Rapid transformation did not occur. Instead, frustration and doubt resulted. Many priests and religious wondered what had gone wrong with renewal. In reality, something was going right: old forms of priestly and religious life were breaking down.

In summary, Catholics are in the midst of a major transition, such as happened only once before in their history. Today's transition can move the Church from a western European to a truly worldwide form, but old religious forms will have to die first. Such painful endings are common during a transition's first phase. Religious professionals, likewise, face significant life changes. Some knowledge of the life cycle of religious orders and congregations will enable us to understand the challenges these men and women confront today.

Life cycle of religious orders and congregations

Like people, religious orders and congregations have a life cycle.[20] The lives of men and women move through alternating times of stability and transition. Group life cycles, however, have these four distinct phases: foundation or institutional origin; expansion; stabilization; and finally, transition.

Period of foundation or institutional origin

First, there is a time of foundation or institutional origin. During this period, usually lasting ten to twenty years or longer, a founding person's vision provides the focus for the life of the religious order or congregation. The founder undergoes a profound personal and religious transformation. Members unite under this person's guidance; a community emerges and searches out vibrant new ways of living the gospel. Together they work toward the realization of God's kingdom.

Marcellin Champagnat saw that the gospel would be unfulfilled unless the rural youth of France were cared for and taught Christ's message of love. Transformed by that vision he founded the Marist Brothers. Ignatius of Loyola had this vision: Christ's teachings needed to be proclaimed loud and clear. He formed a community of companions to accomplish this task. Mother Teresa of Calcutta also has a vision; namely, the dying poor need to be recalled to society's conscience and treated as human beings. Her Missionaries of Charity seek to fulfill this vision of the gospel.

In the life cycle of religious orders and congregations, the period of institutional origin usually coincides with the founding person's final years of life. The community begins to shape its identity, meaning, and purpose. Its vision and energy spring from the founder's charism.

---

20. For a detailed discussion of this topic, see Cada, *Shaping the Coming Age,* pp. 51-113; and Chittister, "Future of Religious Life," pp. 200-203.

Period of expansion

Following the phase of institutional origin, most religious communities experience a fairly lengthy expansion period. It may last for two to three generations or longer. Two outcomes emerge during this period. The energy of the group's members seems endless. Also, the Church and society begin to recognize the group's founding vision and the world's need for it.

At this time the community's sense of mission becomes clear. The founding vision or dream is institutionalized in a variety of ways. If the group's task is to empower people through education, then schools are established. If they fulfill the gospel by treating the sick with dignity, hospitals are erected and staffed. Community policy is fashioned; norms and customs are spelled out. Procedures for decision making, lines of authority, apostolic priorities, and membership qualifications take shape.

The expansion period is an intense time. Members are excited and enthusiastic; large numbers of people join the community; geographic expansion is often rapid; the group documents and interprets its founding vision. Although this period is a dynamic one, rapid growth brings various problems. How does the group maintain its original sense of identity and purpose as it expands? How are rival interpretations of the founding charism to be judged? As these questions emerge, the need to determine the delegation of authority increases. Also, faced with so many challenges and rapid changes, members must be careful not to burn out.

Period of stabilization

The period of stabilization is the third phase of institutional growth. It may be as brief as fifty years or it may last for a century or more. During the stabilization period life gets "tidied up." The group becomes respectable, and its mission gets systematized; the community knows its purpose. Although membership may continue to increase, geographical expansion usually slows.

In the eyes of some, the period of stabilization looks almost problem-free; after all, the group has become socially acceptable. However, the seeds of future discontent are already being sown. Rather than further defining and clarifying the founding vision, the community strives to do better what is already being done. Activism and workaholism often cloud the spiritual and apostolic underpinnings of the work. Furthermore, the community becomes resistant to adaptation as rules begin to take the place of custom; some members play out a status quo "role" as a religious according to society's expectations. Lacking the intensity and vision so characteristic of early community members, many present members are carried along by the group's momentum. A period of transition is needed to rouse the community from its sleep.

Periods of transition

Like a church, transitional phases of religious orders or congregations have three characteristic aspects: breakdown and conflict; darkness and exploration; and reintegration and second foundation.[21]

Breakdown and conflict

The breakdown and conflict phase may develop gradually, lasting a half century or more; it may also be rapid and run its course in just a few decades. During this time, group members become dissatisfied with the current state of the community. They suffer stress as their doubts about the group increase. Morale drops; fewer people are attracted to the community; membership declines through death and the resignation of lifelong members. Examining their recent history, many members of today's religious orders and congregations can recognize these experiences.

Breakdown phases lead to several important consequences. First, the community loses its identity and sense of mission. Institutional structures are dismantled. Members begin to complain about the group's lack of unity. No longer sure what it

---

21. See Cada, *Shaping the Coming Age,* pp. 97-113.

stands for, the community questions its belief system and wonders whether its work is responsive to the signs of the times. Members also wonder if both fulfill the original gospel vision, once the community's focus. Disputes about these concerns lead to polarization. The community is weakened.

Another consequence of the breakdown phase is rising conflicts between the personal needs of members and the group's institutional commitments. Members complain that the community and its apostolic commitments fail to meet their personal and emotional needs. Some decide that religious life is antithetical to their human and religious growth.

Finally, during this phase communication processes and previous decision-making procedures fail. Quite suitable for other phases of the community's life cycle, they are now outdated and fail to take into account the changed nature of the group. Consequently, group members begin to feel incapable of influencing the community's life in any significant manner.

This process of confusion and disintegration, the heart of any group's breakdown phase, signaled the beginning of religious life's present transition. A number of religious, buoyed up with enthusiasm after the Council, were ill-prepared for the situation that developed. Religious communities quickly lost their unifying identity and sense of purpose; their service deteriorated and began to look haphazard and directionless. Former structures were taken apart. Beliefs that had served well during previous stable periods were discarded.

The effects of the transition's first phase can be found in many areas of the lives of today's religious professionals. Consider spirituality. As a number of religious are aware, we live in a period that has witnessed the death of one type of spirituality. Community members used to live a spirituality that was ruled by the clock. Silence was valued; uniformity stressed; singularity rooted out. Religious exercises nourished the spiritual life. God was found in service to others.[22]

---

22. See Martin Helldorfer, "Love: A Need, a Gift, and a Taboo," in *Relationships,* ed. Sean Sammon (Whitinsville, Mass.: Affirmation Books, 1983).

Today fewer and fewer religious are living this type of spirituality. For example, how many still rise at 5:30 A.M. for meditation, followed by community prayer and mass? Spiritual reading in common is not so common anymore. The day no longer ends with evening prayer, particular examen, and the great silence. Many religious and priests have found these changes stressful. They are insecure in the emerging spirituality, which encourages spontaneity and values diversity. It is less concerned with personal perfection than with growth and fulfillment. If the old spirituality forced some individuals into isolation, this new one demands they be relational.

In brief, then, during a transition's first phase groups polarize and a mood of crisis escalates. Familiar authority and decision-making structures erode and "business as usual" ends. Demoralization among group members grows. Feeling as though it is falling apart, listing into disintegration, the group is forced into the transition's middle period of exploration and darkness, aptly named the critical phase.

Darkness and exploration: The critical phase

Antonio Gramsci describes this phase well in his *Prison Notebooks*: "The crisis consists precisely in the fact that the old is dying and the new cannot be born; in this interregnum a great variety of morbid symptoms appear." A group can select one of three options: death, minimal survival, or renewal.[23] For some, the chosen outcome depends upon members' use of the time and opportunities that the critical phase provides. The limitations of other groups may dictate the outcomes available to them.

The transition's first and second phases overlap in a rather messy way. Some of the difficulties in the critical phase are really a reworking of the demands of the breakdown phase to "let go." In real life, phases are never so neatly packaged as they appear theoretically.

For many religious orders and congregations a critical phase lies just ahead. Its possible results are threatening; for instance, some existing orders and congregations may die out during the

---

23. See Chittister, "Future of Religious Life," p. 202.

next several decades. History has many examples: more than 75 percent of the religious orders founded before 1500 no longer exist. Sixty-four percent of those founded before 1800 have also died. It is reasonable to expect that many present-day religious orders will eventually cease to exist. There is nothing inherently wrong with this outcome: building the kingdom of God is important, not the maintenance of orders and congregations. Unfortunately, some contemporary religious professionals appear more earnest about the survival of a school, hospital, or other apostolic work than the message of the gospel. By contrast, founding persons have been generally more concerned with a vision of the gospel and its charismatic expresssion. They have shown significantly less interest in the maintenance of buildings and the security of the group's members.

Some of today's orders and congregations have served their purpose in the Church and have sanctified and transformed many of their members. Currently, however, these groups are unable to read and interpret the signs of the times or they have inadequate resources for renewal. Such groups need to get busy about dying. Although the thought of death is frightening, there is nothing wrong with it. The painful acknowledgment that they have made their final contribution to the Church will allow these groups to plan for their members' welfare and to use their existing resources to the best advantage. Some groups have already begun this process. Greater numbers are merging, and some see individual members transferring to another community. These changes are always difficult. Like Kübler-Ross's patients, many groups at first deny their imminent death, then become angry. Bargaining and depression follow. However, in finally accepting their death, these groups are able to channel their energies creatively and to plan for the future.

Faced with a critical period, other groups that may possess the potential for real renewal choose instead the safety of minimal survival. Dress is modified, language reformed, and community and apostolates restructured. These groups, however, fail to capture religious life's prophetic character. They change but do not renew themselves. Eventually, neither they nor anyone else knows exactly what they stand for. Some of these groups may last, but they will not lead.

What of those groups that choose renewal? For them the critical period is difficult but exciting, the future limitless, not grim. As part of their renewal efforts, these groups address three areas of concern. First, they accept the contradictions that emerged during the breakdown phase. In today's Church these include individual freedom and personal fulfillment versus the group's common goal; personal choice of ministry versus the needs of the community's institutions; and traditional Church work versus response to new needs.[24] By accepting these contradictions the group admits that its present structure and life-style fail to satisfy many members. The community is aware too that its apostolic efforts may no longer be an appropriate response to the needs of the Church and the world. These admissions allow group members to let go of old forms of religious life. Only then can they search out new and vibrant ways of living the gospel.

Second, during the critical phase members need to undergo a personal transformation. This work has several aspects: a new relationship with Jesus; greater depth in faith and prayer; and a genuine openness to the Lord's call. A period of personal darkness and exploration generally precedes this transformation. During this dark night old personal identities and meanings will be lost. Group structures will no longer give a sense of stability and belonging. The experience is similar to being lost in the desert. Like Jacob, people find themselves stripped of the affirmation of society and friends. In wrestling with the angel of their own identity, they pass through their ordeal to a new identity. This process is a normal and necessary aspect of the purification journey. One of its results is a growing awareness that organized efforts are needed to create a more satisfying and genuine community.

This second area of concern is an important one for orders and congregations. The real crisis of religious life today is one of significance and spirituality, not vocations.[25] Consecrated life

---

24. See Cada, *Shaping the Coming Age,* pp. 89-113.
25. See Chittister, "Future of Religious Life," p. 203.

will not survive in a vibrant form unless personal and community prayer come to have a new meaning. In the future, factors such as multiple schedules and individual ministries will challenge any group trying to develop a strong community and prayer life. The challenge should be faced, the obstacles overcome. Otherwise, religious communities will be mere associations and will give little witness to Christ's presence in the world.

Finally, the critical phase gives group members an opportunity to explore variety in their life and work. Through searching and experimentation, they will reach the point where their work and life-style satisfy them and also respond to the needs of the Church and the world. This search will result initially in more failures than successes. Group members need to be comfortable with their mistakes and to learn from them. The search and exploration process has another important outcome: group members rework their institutional charism or dream. This task completed, the charism is freed from the tyranny of its historical trappings and once again gives the community vitality.

For those groups choosing renewal, hope begins to grow as the work of the critical phase proceeds. No master plan, however, helps in this situation. To complete their work successfully, group members need to spend time in the darkness, emptiness, and exploration of the critical phase. Such is the challenge confronting groups seriously interested in renewal today. The time for experimenting and risking is not ending but rather really beginning in a serious manner. The task facing religious orders and congregations, then, is clear: they must mourn their losses and pursue experimentation and risk-taking by surrendering to the darkness and emptiness of the transition's critical phase.

Reintegration and a new foundation

For several reasons, personal transformation among a significant number of group members is the prime mover in the transition's final phase. First, conversion reorients members as their perceptions change. They develop new insights into the contemporary world and its problems. Members also make a commitment to a new way of acting, and the nature of their life changes.

Furthermore, transformed members are more sensitive to the needs of the materially poor. Their prayer life is more innovative, and they acquire greater understanding of spiritual growth. This process of transformation is difficult and slow.

For the group to be truly revitalized, transformation must move beyond the personal. Renewed members start this process by forming relationship networks to support their new awareness. New ventures in ministry or life-style sometimes accompany the formation of these networks. Leadership support is important for the success of such ventures. Eventually, these relationship networks animate the larger group, and community experiences become more rewarding. Evangelical discipleship is gripping and the group begins to write a new chapter of its history.

Many religious orders and congregations today have the necessary resources to renew themselves. They have the same challenge as the rich young man of the gospels. This man of great wealth came to Jesus with a question: "What is still necessary for me to do in order to possess eternal life?" Although the man had kept all the commandments since his youth, Jesus saw beyond his lifelong practice of the Law. This man was obedient, but his practice of religion was superficial. Jesus spoke to the man. To possess eternal life, he would have to sacrifice his great wealth. The story's end is well known. The young man failed to accept the invitation to renew himself. He remained isolated in his righteousness. He decided against vitality, a new life, a second foundation. He also went away sad.

Thus, those groups that renew themselves will accomplish three tasks: they will rediscover their original charism; they will listen to and interpret the signs of their times; and their members will undergo conversion and develop prayerful lives centered in Christ.[26]

In summary, throughout the history of religious life, transitions are evident. They take a common form: breakdown; search and exploration; reintegration and foundation. Our present transition is no different. During it some groups may die, but

---

26. See Cada, *Shaping the Coming Age,* pp. 89-113.

religious life itself will survive. What looks like an ending today is instead an invitation to recreate a new image of religious life.

Religious life's dominant image

During a particular historical period, the dominant image of religious life is the one that best captures members' view of their life and ministry within the Church.[27] The history of religious life shows that down through the centuries at least five images have successfully caught the dominant focus of what religious life was all about: the ages of the desert, monasticism, the mendicants, the apostolic orders, and, more recently, the service congregations. Today's transition will bring a new dominant image of religious life. Its genuineness will be judged by two factors: its ability to inspire people, and its success in encompassing the ideal to which religious aspire. A look at the familiar image of the service congregations illustrates the presence of these two factors in the past.

The age of the service congregations

The period from 1800 until the present has seen the foundation of more than 600 new congregations. In addition, older groups such as the Jesuits and the Dominicans have been rejuvenated in the image of the new service congregations. In this age of the service congregations, institutions have been built and staffed. Life-style has been a blend of personal holiness and active apostolic service. Members have sought both their own salvation and that of others. The number of religious increased to its greatest size in history during this age, peaking about the time of the Second Vatican Council. But now, to renew itself, religious life needs a new dominant image. Before speculating about the structure of that image, we need more information about the history of religious life.

The age of the desert

The age of the desert lasted from approximately 200 A.D. through 500 A.D. During this period, religious were holy ascetics.

---

27. For more detailed information on the evolution of religious life, see ibid., pp. 11-50.

They withdrew into the desert to serve the Church by doing battle with the devil. Living as hermits or gathering together in monasteries under a master, desert monks returned to society periodically. Their power to do good was manifested in healing the sick, comforting the sorrowful, and casting out demons. Even today, the desert image evokes a spiritual meaning, for prayer and mortification are important to it. Stated simply, nothing in the world is worth putting ahead of the Lord. Although no longer its dominant image, the age of the desert made a permanent contribution to religious life.

The age of monasticism

Between approximately 500 A.D. and 1200 A.D., monastery life under the holy rule's discipline was the ideal image of religious life. Unceasing praise of God was its goal; daily liturgical prayer, work, and contemplation provided the means to attain it. Monastic nuns and monks also provided an example to their society of deep spirituality combined with loving ministry to one's neighbor. As some monasteries became little more than feudal estates, however, twelfth-century religious life began to grope for a new image. The rise of the mendicants rewarded this search.

The age of the mendicants

The age of the mendicants ran from approximately 1200 A.D. through 1500 A.D. Unencumbered by wealth and property, mendicants observed the gospel injunction to give their possessions to the poor. Begging for their keep, these simple friars preached, served the poor, cultivated learning, and traveled wherever their Church had needs. In time, though, many members of these groups succumbed to the very evils that had brought about their original flowering: wealth and the good life. Religious life again needed a reformation. It came with the rise of the apostolic orders.

The age of the apostolic orders

Lasting from approximately 1500 A.D. through 1800 A.D., the age of the apostolic orders provided the Church with an elite corps of men and women to address the Counter-Reformation's formidable challenge. These emerging groups provided charitable and educational services. They also reinforced the Church's political power throughout Catholic Europe and preached the gospel in foreign missions. Lacking the support of monastic observances, members of the apostolic orders relied on a high level of personal holiness in facing the risks of their new undertakings.

Religious life's new dominant image

Despite the gloomy picture, religious life is not dead; however, it has been falling asleep. The current transition period is needed for this life-style to reflect anew the gospel message. What about the future? Although no one can predict it accurately, patterns can be observed, trends assessed, and speculations advanced. Indications are that the number of people in religious life will be smaller, the membership older. Community life and prayer probably will take exciting new forms. Ministry will, in many cases, arise out of present needs rather than historical commitments. As a consequence, religious life may be less institutional, with communities based on relationships rather than work. Distinctions between different orders and congregations will probably be less clear as members mix in living situations and ministry. As in times past, transition has roused many religious groups from their sleep. For some, it has been a rude awakening.

Transitions in priesthood

Our image of priesthood is also in transition. At one time, everyone knew what the word meant. Today, people are not so sure. There is the ordained priesthood; but, then again, what about the priesthood of all the faithful? In the past, ordination gave a man the fullness of ministry. More recently baptism has taken priority. Priesthood once again is moving through a period of change and development.[28]

Evolution of the term "priest"

According to the New Testament, only Christ and the Christian community are priestly. While leaders are at the service of Christ and God's priestly people, they themselves are never said to be priestly.[29] Historically, then, early Christians avoided using the term "priest." They never applied it to any Christian, even the twelve apostles. For them there was but one priest: Jesus. In the New Testament, the term is confined almost exclusively to the letter to the Hebrews, where it applies to the Lord. Even in Hebrews, however, "priest" is used in a special way. Coming out of neither the Levitical tradition nor the ancient line of Aaron or Zadoc, Jesus is not a traditional priest. He is a priest in the line of Melchizedek.[30]

The Pharisaical movement of Judaism influenced the shape of Jesus' priestly role. A new religious figure had emerged from this movement: the scribe, later called the rabbi. Neither prophet nor priest, his domain was equally the synagogue and the marketplace. The rabbi had two roles: everyday interpreter of the Law; and an in-the-field minister of mercy, healing, and good works. In time the rabbi came to replace the priest as the chief symbol of Jewish commitment.[31]

Jesus was a rabbi. He explained and applied the Law to daily practical situations, showed mercy, healed, and practiced good works. This image of the rabbi also strongly affected the shape of the Christian Church and its concept of ministry. The primacy of public ministry over the cultic priesthood was affirmed

---

28. Two excellent sources of information on the evolution of the priesthood are Bausch, *Traditions,* and Edward Schillebeeckx, *Ministry: Leadership in the Community of Jesus Christ,* trans. John Bowden (New York: Crossroads, 1981). The material for this discussion on transitions in the priesthood is drawn from these two sources.

29. Schillebeeckx, *Ministry,* p. 48.

30. Bausch, *Traditions,* pp. 31-32, and Schillebeeckx, *Ministry,* p. 33.

31. Bausch, *Traditions,* pp. 38-39.

in the daily life of the Church. Stated simply, first-century Christianity was clearly a Christianity of interpretation of the Law and service, not of cult and priesthood.[32]

By the fourth century, however, a fairly well-defined and confined concept of the priest applied to individual Christians. What caused this change? How did it happen?

Who presided at the eucharist?

One way to chart early changes in the meaning of priesthood is to answer this question: prior to the introduction of the formal office of priest, who precisely presided at the eucharist? Apparently, a number of different people did. The early eucharist took its form from the Jewish grace at meals—the *birkat hamazon.* Everyone was not eligible to preside in this situation. So also, not all believers could preside at the eucharist, but only a person who was competent to lead the community. Although the New Testament tells us little about the situation, in the early centuries of Christianity prophets and teachers definitely presided at the eucharist. If they were not available, bishops and deacons were eligible, not because they were deacons and bishops but because "they too fulfill among you the office of prophet and teacher."

This presiding role expanded later to include others. Clement of Rome tells us that eminent men could preside with the consent of the whole Church. Even after the office of priest was established, others continued to preside. Tertullian suggested that a layman could do so in the absence of an ordained priest. The *Apostolic Witness of Hippolytus* mentions confessors presiding at the eucharist, the almost-martyrs who were imprisoned, tortured, and nearly killed for the faith. Their bravery and endurance qualified them as prophets and teachers—natural leaders of the community, entitled to preside at the eucharist.[33] In 314 A.D.

---

32. Ibid., p. 39.

33. Ibid., pp. 34-36, and Schillebeeckx, *Ministry,* pp. 30; 48-52. Tertullian stated: "But where no college of ministers has been appointed, you, the laity, must celebrate the eucharist and baptize; in that case you are your own priests, for where two or three are gathered together, there is the Church, even if these three are lay people."

the Council of Arles decided that during the persecution of Diocletian, in the absence of a priest, deacons might preside at the eucharist in an emergency. In the minds of first-century Christians, however, being a prophet and teacher, a natural leader of the community, entitled one to preside.[34] This role was not tied in with the personal power of the individual nor personal priestly characteristics. Rather, it grew out of one's role as president of the community.

The logic behind this notion is compelling. To preside means to gather into one, to unify, and to encourage. This concept finds its highest expression in the eucharist—a celebration of unity, service, and fellowship.

Throughout the New Testament, leadership is service or *diakonia*. In the early Christian community, the leader's primary role was to build up the community, not to be an intermediary between humankind and God. "Priestliness," the offering up of sanctified lives and work to the Father, was not confined to any one individual. Instead, all baptized persons were priestly. In the early Christian community no one was given this special status: the Spirit was poured out upon all. The equality is evident in the diversity of gifts, roles, and charisms mentioned in 1 Corinthians (1 Cor. 12:4-5, 28). Ephesians also mentions these five ministries: apostle, prophet, teacher, evangelist, and pastor (Eph. 4:11-14). Finally, in Acts Luke reports that the community was close-knit. Members prayed, held things in common, proclaimed the word of the Lord, reached out to those in need, and broke bread together (Acts 2:42, 44-47).

As the Church moved beyond its first century, the community's role in the eucharist remained central. Even when people were ordained, it was primarily to build up and celebrate community. Only then did they preside at the eucharist. The reverse was never true. One was not ordained to preside at the eucharist and then, as a side effect, preside over the community. The Council of Chalcedon in the fourth century, for example, specifically forbade anyone to be ordained without first having a

---

34. Bausch, *Traditions*, p. 35.

community.[35] Ancient canons voided the ordination of anyone who was a free-floating presider of the eucharist without a community. Such a situation was seen as a contradiction.

As the eucharist became more cultic and Old Testament concepts of sacrifice were applied, an elaborate liturgy was spun around it. A priest rather than a presider was called for. Other changes followed. With the notion of sacrifice prevailing, it became logical to have the eucharistic meal take place in a temple. The table became an altar, the bishop both high priest and mediator between God and humankind. Although these changes happened slowly, they were well entrenched by the third and fourth centuries. By then the word "priest" had become attached to an individual Christian, the bishop, and to him alone. In summary, though no cultic priesthood appears in the New Testament, the Church eventually imported Old Testament Levitical forms and imposed them on Christian ministry.

It is difficult to determine just what caused Christianity to return to the old Judaic notions of cultic priesthood. In so doing, it rejected the more recent notion of scribe and rabbi springing out of the Pharisaical movement. Perhaps the change was set in motion by Christianity's rapid expansion into the gentile world, where anti-Semitism would not accept Christianity's current forms. Also, Gentiles were more familiar with the concept of sacrifice; their pagan priests were familiar symbols of power.[36] In making these changes, the Christian community was moving toward a time when a priest would be ordained to offer mass. This concept, however, was a departure from the original tradition.

We know, then, that the title "priest" was first applied to the bishop. How was it transferred from the bishop to the priest we know today? The change was relatively simple. Bishops were always based in urban areas. The Council of Laodicea legislated this situation by decreeing that bishops were needed in the large city centers and therefore did not belong in the countryside

---

35. Bausch, *Traditions,* p. 45, and Schillebeeckx, *Ministry,* pp. 38-41, 52.

36. Bausch, *Traditions,* pp. 40-41.

(canon 57). As Christianity spread rapidly, bishops were unable to oversee the far-flung communities springing up throughout the countryside. For help, bishops turned to elder-presbyters who already were presiding over the local communities. An old principle was reinstated: he who presides over the community also presides at the eucharist. The presbyter received the title of priest. At first, this transfer was made without benefit of a special ordination. The presbyter-priest was now the bishop's delegate, a concept that continues today. The bishop, though, most often kept the tasks of initiation, confirmation, reconciliation, jurisdiction, and teaching to himself. Little was left to the priest other than to be a minister of the eucharist. Priests, then, inherited the bishop's altar-presiding role when the latter became too busy to take care of the outlying districts under his jurisdiction. Eventually the role of priest began to shift from one of service to one of status.[37]

The Catholic priest of today is really the Jewish elder-presbyter of yesterday. These men were installed in their position by the laying on of hands; their tasks included judging, guiding, and presiding over the local community. Sent out from the Jerusalem Sanhedrin, Jewish elder-presbyters traveled as apostles. They brought judgment, redressed wrongs, and formed liaisons with local governments.

Other important historical factors have contributed to the evolution of priesthood's image. In the twelfth century, the Third Lateran Council decreed that unless assured of a proper living, a man should not be ordained. Here was a shift in emphasis: rather than have a community call him to service, a man needed a community to support him financially. Pope Innocent I, during the early fifth century, had already ruled that a man could be ordained without a community if his bishop would at least provide for him financially. Note that with these developments, ordination was no longer tied into presidency of the local community. Instead, it imparted a personal investment of power that could be carried anywhere. Associated now with personal power, ordination lost its community roots. The Fourth Lateran

---

37. Ibid., pp. 41-42, and Schillebeeckx, *Ministry,* pp. 48-49.

Council in the thirteenth century clarified the nature and extent of this personal power by specifying that the eucharist could be celebrated only by a validly ordained priest.[38]

With this awesome personal power, the priest also became something of a sacred person, a man apart. In being ordained he received a "mark," the "character" of priesthood. A sacred person with personal power, he could also do something that to the early Christians was inconceivable: offer a private mass.

Being a sacred person, though, had its consequences. Priests were warned to keep their distance from defiling secular occupations. As the analogy grew between Levitical priests of the Old Law and Christian priests of the New Law, so did the notion of Levitical purity, marking the beginning of a move toward priestly celibacy. When serving in the temple, the priests of the Old Law had abstained from sexual relations with their wives. The notion of abstinence for priests of the New Law was rooted in this practice. The law of celibacy was promulgated explicitly in canons six and seven of the Second Lateran Council in 1139 as an attempt to make the law of abstinence effective.[39] This decision, concluding a long history in which there was simply a law of abstinence that applied to married priests, needs some explanation.

In both the New Testament and the early Church there were both married and unmarried priests. Those who chose to remain unmarried did so for personal, social, or religious reasons. During the first centuries of the Church, an increasing number of priests remained unmarried. They did so freely, their decision inspired by the same motives as those of monks. In the Eastern and Western Churches of the first ten centuries, then, both married and unmarried men were welcomed as priests. Celibacy was not a requirement for entering ministry. Toward the end of the fourth century, though, legislation appeared in the Western Church regarding married priests. Rooted in notions of ritual purity, it took the form of the law of abstinence. Stated simply,

---

38. Bausch, *Traditions,* pp. 45-47.
39. Schillebeeckx, *Ministry,* p. 85.

sexual intercourse was forbidden the night before communicating at eucharist. Although this custom had long been observed in the Church, its practice became something of a problem when the Western Churches began to celebrate daily eucharist. At that time, abstinence became a permanent condition for married priests.[40] To enforce this situation a law became necessary. Such canonical legislation however, was not a law of celibacy but a law of abstinence connected with ritual purity and focused on the eucharist.

There were several reasons for returning to old notions of ritual purity. First of all, laws of purity for pagan priests were quite prominent in the Mediterranean areas. Second, there was the influence of the Stoical ideal of "equanimity." According to this notion, sexual intercourse was a "little epilepsy." Thought to rob people of their senses, it was therefore not in accord with reason. Finally, Neo-Pythagorean thought and later Neo-Platonic dualism played an important part. Influencing the law of abstinence and the later law of celibacy, then, is an antiquated anthropology and a questionable view of sexuality.[41] More important, though, the law of celibacy was really a drastic attempt to make the law of abstinence effective. This discipline was being observed only superficially by married priests; to enforce it the Second Lateran Council declared marriage to be a bar to priesthood. From 1139 A.D. onwards, only the unmarried could be ordained.

I am not attempting to discredit celibacy by examining its historical roots in the Western Church. A number of Church ministers choose celibacy freely and experience it as a charism. However, contemporary discussions of committed celibacy and its place in the Church need to be informed not only by theological and spiritual understandings but also by historical facts, and a contemporary anthropology and understanding of human sexuality.

Some centuries later the thought of Josse Clichtove greatly influenced the Council of Trent's understanding of the image of

---

40. Ibid., pp. 85-89.
41. Ibid., p. 88.

priest. He argued that by virtue of his state in life, the priest is detached from the world. This image of the priesthood was once again influenced by the Old Testament's Levitical priestly laws as well as the traditions of monastic life. Stated simply, priesthood was defined by its relationship to cult and not to community. Being cultic priests, ministers had little to do with people, even their own parishioners, except for sacramental work. The priest was set apart, and celibacy was the only adequate sign of this important separation. Edward Schillebeeckx summarizes Clichtove's notions about celibacy:

> Celibacy, regarded solely as restraint from what Clichtove calls fleshly impurity (*spurcitia*), is the "*claustrum*" that cuts off the priest from the world and segregates him. To give permission to the priest to marry would be equivalent to blurring the distinction between layman and priest. The whole of Clichtove's view is based on the supremely sacred power of the priest to offer sacrifice. Therefore "religion" *par excellence* belongs to the caste of the priests and monks, who are far above the ordinary believers. Precisely on the basis of this power to offer sacrifice the priest is the mediator between God and believers.[42]

While Trent avoided his exaggerations, the influence of Clichtove's ideas can be seen in the "French school" of priestly formation that shaped much of the background for the spiritual literature about priesthood in recent centuries. Furthermore, the influence of Clichtove's questionable outlook is evident in many seminary training programs even into the present century. It is against this backdrop that today's Catholic Church carries out its attempts to renew priestly life.

Contemporary Catholic priesthood is struggling for a new identity. This is a healthy development. For a long period the priest's role has been too narrowly defined and in need of expansion. Actually, there are at least five distinct priestly roles. The juridical role emphasizes the priest as one who holds full authority from the bishop and also teaches with authority. The cultic role, popular during medieval times, sees the priest largely in terms of performing the sacred mysteries. In a pastoral role,

42. Ibid., p. 59.

the priest is primarily the community leader and healer. As a prophet the priest is the mighty proclaimer of God's word. Finally, in the monastic role the priest is the holy one, the guru, the spiritual director of souls. Thus the rich meaning of priesthood, much wider than the altar-oriented, cultic connotation of recent years, needs to be reclaimed.[43]

As a consequencè of the evolution of the priesthood into a separate and sacred class, a caste system was created within the Church. Official ministry, serving the mission of the Church and referring to the service of the community that keeps the gospel alive and tradition intact, became the exclusive domain of the clergy.[44] Lay men and women in ministry were generally clericalized. For example, the original lay ministries of subdeacon, exorcist, porter, and acolyte were established as steps toward ordination. In many religious orders, men were ordained priests even if they rarely celebrated mass. In our own century, Pius XII called the work of the laity "Catholic Action." Officially, the term meant "the participation of the laity in the apostolate of the hierarchy." The message is clear: ministry belongs to the hierarchy.

Today this notion of ministry is beginning to change as the Church returns to the original meaning: the priestly and prophetic work of the Church.[45] Because ministries are detached from the clerical office and redistributed among the community, the terms ministry and office are sometimes thought to be opposed. The early Church saw no such opposition. For them, office was a ministerial charism that was institutionalized. All God's people are called to preserve tradition, gather the community, and celebrate ritual. They also need to speak God's word boldly and serve the needs of others.

Ministry will have a difficult transition. Many religious professionals, for example, have felt a loss as their apostolates

---

43. See Walter J. Burghardt, "What Is a Priest?" *The Way,* supplement no. 23 (Autumn 1974).

44. Bausch, *Traditions,* pp. 11-26.

45. Maria Harris, *Portrait of Youth Ministry* (Ramsey, N.J.: Paulist Press, 1981), p. 13.

opened to a wider variety of Christians. A number of religious orders and dioceses have also been reluctant to open decision-making roles to laity. Some pastors feel threatened by parish councils and the presence of religious sisters, brothers, and other lay men and women on their parish staffs. This reluctance and fear and the accompanying confusion are often characteristic of a transition's first phase and are to be expected as old Church forms break down.

Conclusion

The Chinese were right. A transitional age is a curse. Old forms break down and die out. People feel confused, frightened, even overwhelmed. This bad news seems to get worse as a group moves into its critical period. Members make mistakes and sometimes believe that they were better off with what they had before. The period is one of genuine crisis. As such it is also a turning point, a time of decision.

Today, compelling evidence exists that the Church, priesthood, and religious orders and congregations are in the midst of major transitions. Such periods of change and upheaval have occurred at various times in the history of the Church. Stress is greater, however, when they take place in all three groups simultaneously.

For at least the past two decades, Church members, priests, and religious have experienced breakdown and confusion in the familiar and once stable structure of their committed life-styles. A number of people are frightened about what this situation might mean for their future. The expected period of renewal has not come to pass. In some circles, there is thought of returning to previous forms and regret that any changes were made in the first place. To move in these directions is to miss the point of our present period of transition and also to deny Church history. Ours is not the first age of transition in the Church; surely it will not be the last. We are privileged to live in these crisis times when we can contribute to creating a new image of the Church, religious life, and priesthood.

Every crisis is a time of danger but also of opportunity. Today we can begin anew in the Church, priesthood, and religious life. The danger is that we will refuse to pay the necessary price, namely, loss of our old forms and understandings. When the People of God finally reach their new beginning, they will realize that it was indeed a small price to pay.

As the transition in the Church and among priests and religious has affected styles of life, notions about government, law, and authority, the practice of prayer, and life in community, so also has American society's present period of change, upheaval, and growth had its effects on these institutions. In the next chapter I will examine America's social revolution and evaluate its impact on Church life and the practice of leadership.

Chapter Three

The new American revolution

America's social fabric is changing. Today, nearly half of all marriages end in divorce; 40 percent of all children born in this decade will spend part of their youth in single parent households; the number of unmarried couples living together has more than doubled since 1960. The mobility of many Americans is also evident. Twenty percent of all families in the country move each year, with the average homeowner staying in a single home for about seven years.[1] We also live in an age of technology. Not only did *Time* magazine's editors name the personal computer "Man of the Year" in 1982, but since that time a second generation of personal computers has appeared on the American scene. Having moved into our homes, these well-crafted pieces of technology are changing our lives.

America's technological accomplishments have always influenced the social, cultural, and religious fabric of its society. Consider the past century. Advances in transportation, communication, and media changed the way Americans live. The western frontier closed in 1890. About the same time, electricity did away with the day in rhythm with the sun. Telephones replaced the telegraph. Air transportation began in 1910, just shortly after the Wright brothers' first flight, and before long it challenged the supremacy of the rails in speedy and efficient travel. More recently, newspaper readers defected and now seek their information from radio and television.

---

1. See Keith W. Sehnert, *Stress/Unstress* (Minneapolis: Augsburg, 1981).

71

These advances have significantly changed life in the United States. The telephone, for example, brought into question conventional understandings of friendship and intimacy. Prior to its introduction, relationships depended, for the most part, on the physical proximity of people. Now they can be maintained across continents. In a geographically mobile society like America the telephone has helped people preserve deep friendships, even at a distance. This advance, however, brings with it at least one danger: people may treat their local environment with contempt. Having friends "all over the country," men and women may not be so attentive to their neighbors next door.[2]

The Catholic Church in the United States, religious life, and the priesthood have not escaped the influence of technology's advances. Here also, change was rapid and far-reaching. For example, in 1890 the immigrant Church was wary of America. Many of its members planned to return to their homelands. Rather than "fitting in," Catholics were outsiders. Today, few would argue that the American Church is in the mainstream. Communications systems speed the exchange of Church information. A television satellite is used to spread the gospel message. Catholic educational and health institutions boast of the latest technical equipment. Technology also influenced religious life-styles. The media's invasion of the monastery caused an information explosion. No longer confined to the cloister or semicloistered living situations, priests and religious became citizens of the global village. Within religious orders and con-

---

2. See John Staudermaier, S.J.'s excellent analysis entitled "Technology and Culture in the U.S.: 1950 to the Present—A Time of Upheaval," in the proceedings of the 1981 Religious Formation Conference's National Conference. (For copies write to the Conference, 1234 Massachusetts Avenue, N.W., Washington, D.C. 20005). For more information on Americans' attitudes toward themselves, their work, their families, and the remedies they seek to problems, see Joseph Veroff, Elizabeth Douvan, and Richard A. Kulka, *The Inner American: A Self-Portrait from 1957 to 1976* (New York: Basic Books, 1981), as well as Mary Douglas, "The Effects of Modernization on Religious Change," *Daedalus* III, no. 1 (Winter 1982): 1-20.

gregations and dioceses, technology keeps members mobile, comfortable, and informed. No longer thinking of itself as alien, an immigrant, the Church has instead become an insider.

Is all this progress in Church institutions and society a blessing? In spite of recent technological advances, many people question the health of contemporary American society. They cite the assassinations of recent years, the Vietnam War, duplicity in government, and apathy among the citizenry.[3] Is American society sick? Have its people become more self-involved and selfish? The answers to these questions have important implications for the Church and religious and priestly life, for religious professionals and other Church members are influenced by society's values, traits, and attitudes. If American society is sick, what influence does this have on the Church, religious life, and priesthood? Also, what of the young men and women considering religious and priestly life today? How have America's technological advances and its changing social and religious fabric influenced them?

Understanding today's transition in the Church, priesthood, and religious life requires an awareness of the general impact of recent social, cultural, and technological change in America. In particular, it is necessary to grasp the effect of these factors on priests and religious and their views of authority and leadership within the Church. To accomplish these tasks, I will first examine the evolution of America's social character, paying particular attention to the country's present character. Next, I will identify the social, cultural, and technological trends that shaped this new character and examine the latter's influence on Church life and leadership.

The evolution of America's social character

The term "character" describes a person's values, traits, and attitudes. A young man's character, for example, can be judged

---

3. See Christopher Lasch, *The Culture of Narcissism* (New York: W. W. Norton, 1979).

as "generous," "mean," "curious," or "duplicitous." Psychologist Michael MacCoby suggests that any group of people also has a character, a social character.[4] It describes their best and worst traits as a group.

Social commentators have used a variety of images to define Americans' values and traits. In 1831 Alexis de Tocqueville described the individualistic rights-conscious character of the American nation. It was, he said, built on the principle of equality by farmers and craftspeople who believed in the infinite perfectibility of human beings. Over a century later, young Americans of the 1950s were characterized as a "Silent Generation" of unquestioning conformers. Throughout the country's history, five distinct social characters captured America's best and worst traits.

The Puritan ethic

America's first social character was dominated by the seventeenth-century Puritan or Protestant ethic. It expressed Calvinist and Quaker individualism and asceticism, was antagonistic to sensuality, and reinforced rigid self-discipline and deferral of rewards. "Trust no one," the Puritans warned; one's only confidant should be God.

The craft ethic

The craft ethic, popularized by Ben Franklin's "poor Richard" Saunders, espoused the virtues of temperance, resolution, sincerity, frugality, moderation, and chastity. Unlike the Puritan, Franklin's craftsman no longer worked for God's glory but for himslef. "God helps those who help themselves," he advised. The craft ethic had a number of positive traits, each with its negative counterpart. Frugality can lead to stinginess, resolution and rugged individualism to obstinacy. Useful during an age of economic and technological independence, the craft ethic lost favor in time.

---

4. See Michael MacCoby's *The Leader* (New York: Simon and Schuster, 1981) for an analysis of American social character, pp. 13-55.

The entrepreneurial ethic

As the nineteenth century began, frontier expansion and the Industrial Revolution fueled people's dreams. The moderation and cautiousness of Franklin's craftsman was replaced by the entrepreneur's daring and speculation. The Horatio Alger myth and the entrepreneurial ethic were born. Skilled and tough, the entrepreneur built industries and survived in a competitive jungle. He could also be greedy, exploitative, and domineering.

The career ethic

More recently, prompted by social changes, a career ethic replaced the older Puritan, craft, and entreprencurial ethics. In the late nineteenth and early twentieth centuries, more and more Americans left their rural, craft-based societies to educate themselves for life and to work within large organizations. They were willing to sacrifice their personal development and fulfillment for institutional needs.

The new ethic exacted its toll. People felt uprooted, many becoming dependent upon organizations for their identity. Social critics questioned the cost of the new ethic.[5] Fearing it would undermine the spiritual traditions of Western civilization, they blamed it for producing a bland, conformist, and soulless society.

John Kennedy's presidency illustrates the kind of leadership that came with the career ethic. He displayed a "gamesman" style of leadership, marked by boyish informality and the enjoyment of give-and-take.[6] He controlled subordinates by persuasion, enthusiasm, and the promise of success.

---

5. Walter Lippman said, "The school must sink, therefore, into being a mere training ground for personal careers. Its object must then be to equip individual careerists and not to form fully civilized men" (in "The State of Education in This Troubled Age," annual meeting of the American Association for the Advancement of Science, Philadelphia, December 29, 1940). See also William H. Whyte, *The Organization Man* (New York: Simon and Schuster, 1956).

6. See Michael MacCoby, *The Gamesman* (New York: Simon and Schuster, 1976).

By the late 1970s, however, this gamesman style of leadership no longer brought out the best in America's unstable social character. The country's population was older, its resources limited. A new era dawned and a new ethic began to emerge.

The self-development ethic

Three interweaving currents have been transforming America's national character since the craft and entrepreneurial eras, with significant implications for priestly, religious, and Church life. To begin with, America's technological revolution created a postindustrial society that led to many changes. Communications grew exponentially, allowing the instantaneous transmission of information, making large interdependent organizations possible, and challenging previous understandings of intimacy. During the last century, Americans were pleased that the telegraph enabled them to learn of breaking news within a day's time. In recent years, same-day television coverage of events has become commonplace. Worldwide telecommunications systems expedite the flow of information between international corporations. Mass media and the telephone shrink the distance between friends.

As communications systems grew, Church members were exposed to new ideas and many people developed a desire for learning. Consequently, old outlooks and understandings in priestly and religious life were called into question as increasing numbers of priests, sisters, and brothers were educated outside of parochial institutions.

The new technology also challenged the Church's traditional moral code. It encouraged new ideas and questioned old taboos. For example, the technology of birth control confronted the Church's sexual morality and contributed to a new sexual revolution. The ascetic character that gave emotional conviction to the Puritan and craft ethics was formed by a repressive moral code that today has lost its force. This fact coupled with the media's message to consume rather than save releases many of those restraints that structured the traditional character of and moral authority within religious life. This situation is also evident in society. Adults of all classes break old taboos and pursue possessions and experiences of food, travel, and entertainment that in the past were available only to the wealthy.[7]

America's movement from a rural, craft-based society to a semi-urban one generated a second transforming influence on its character. Employed by large corporations, more and more people developed new definitions of work. A sense of self was no longer based on self-employment, family, and place. A personal sense of identity was no longer given but, instead, had to be created by each person.

Religious professionals face a similar struggle for identity in moving from an institutional understanding of ministry to a more personal one. Place of ministry no longer provides relationships and a sense of identity. Instead, many priests, brothers, and sisters are forced to create and develop new identities and ways of relating. Their level of psychological and emotional development makes this task extremely stressful for some. Others, however, enjoy the challenge of possible growth, intent on liberating themselves from their emotional and social insularism. In the past, their personal growth might have been suspended or delayed through personal decisions or life circumstances. Now, however, these men and women have a sense of purpose and a strong desire to move forward in their personal development. A number of experiences may have brought them to this point: a new job or ministry assignment, new educational experiences, the effects of Vatican II, a serious failure, or profound religious or personal changes. The personal experience of change is the most potent and frequent force reinitiating growth and leading to a new identity in the lives of religious professionals.

A third current shaping the self-development character is the recent challenge to paternal authority. The student protest and antiwar movements of the 1960s questioned traditional notions of authority. As a result, there is a new distrust of any power or authority that might limit self-expression. Parents, popes,

---

7. MacCoby, *The Leader,* p. 40.

priests, presidents, provincials, and professors are no longer guaranteed deference.

Today, power attracts few young people. Neither will they defer to it. A large number of them want neither to lead nor to follow. Rather, they seek interesting work and satisfying emotional relationships.

The women's movement has provided another challenge to paternal authority. The myth of male superiority has been questioned and its foundations shaken.

Both the student and the women's movements have dulled the past attraction of Church power. Religious people looking for interesting ministry are no longer willing to purchase it at the price of a full emotional life. Religious professionals in increasing numbers are deciding against ministries that lack opportunities for critical thinking, self-expression, and growth. The resulting crisis in Church authority challenges the institutional commitments and priorities of many groups.

In summary, the new social character evolving today is more oriented to the self and its expression than to craft, enterprise, career, or institution. Because its influence is felt in our contemporary Church, a full description of this character and its implications for Church life and leadership is called for.

The social character of today: Self-development

The new self-development ethic, like previous ones, has both positive and negative aspects. On the positive side, it promotes experimentation, flexibility, and tolerance. Doubting the value of roles and status, people espousing this ethic are willing to experiment with new relationships in ministry and personal life. Loyalty to organizations in the traditional sense of submission and self-sacrifice is not a priority. The new ethic does not encourage following orders blindly. Instead, it demands good reasons for decisions and believes in justice and participative decision making. At its best, it cultivates playfulness and is oriented toward development of self and other people in the areas of health, lifelong learning, and enriching experiences. Stated simply, the person shaped by the self-development ethic says to society and Church authorities: "I can contribute more if you will listen to my ideas, relate to me as an individual, and treat me fairly. *If you don't I'll just have to look out for myself.''*

In view of this description, some critics charge that the new ethic is a negative one and that Americans have lost their traditional values and become self-indulgent.[8] Religious superiors worry that some of their group members are becoming rebellious, demanding, self-serving, and manipulative. Does the self-development ethic promote narcissism? If so, what does this imply for the priesthood, religious life, and the exercise of Church leadership?

To answer these questions, we must first define egocentrism, narcissism, and egoism. All three terms describe people who are uncaring and have little concern about the well-being of others. Egocentrism and narcissism are developmental problems, whereas egoism is a moral choice. If we confuse these three terms we draw false conclusions about America's new social character.

Egocentrism is a cognitive orientation common in young children. Because they are self-centered, young children cannot take another person's point of view. Instead, they regard everything in relation to themselves. Egocentric children explain the world in terms of adult authority. Egocentric adults, appearing childish and dependent, are unable to empathize with others or to reflect on their own behavior. They are uncritical of authority. Rather, by internalizing the views of authority, they give meaning and direction to their own behavior. During transitional times egocentric men and women experience considerable stress.

Most people evidence some strong narcissistic tendencies during adolescence. Pathological narcissism is different: it is an emotional disturbance. Narcissistic people direct love away from other people and toward their own body, talents, prestige, or goodness. The disorder can be classified into two categories: primary and secondary. Primary narcissism is marked by extreme megalomania and loss of touch with reality. Secondary narcissism is a higher level of emotional development where love is

---

8. See Lasch, *Culture of Narcissism.*

withdrawn from others and focused on an idealized self. Narcissists are generally unhappy because they are unable to be empathetic or to care about others. People are real to narcissists only as they are for or against them.

Today many people, including a number of religious professionals, are concerned with satisfaction at work, spiritual experience, their personal and educational development, and health. Does this mean that they are troubled with a pathological disorder? Probably not. It might imply that they are taking mature responsibility for their health and well-being and are less inclined to submit to experts and "saviors." However, when Church people feel that authority does not consult with them, many will turn defensively to egoism.

Egoism, a moral choice, is a defensive reaction used by insecure people when they fear the loss of their identity. Stated simply, they decide to look out for themselves. This solution enables them to keep their self-esteem and identity as they attempt to adapt and become what others want them to be. Egoism is neither arrested development nor psychopathology; rather, it is the defensive choice of many Americans who feel they are losing part of themselves in their attempts to adapt and ingratiate, to be what others want, to become more marketable. The success of programs such as *est* and books peddling a "look out for number one" philosophy of life is due, for the most part, to the fear of insecure Americans who feel they are losing a sense of self by overadapting themselves. To counteract this fear, many people are attracted to programs and ideas that encourage them to stop feeling and acting like a powerless cog in a wheel, to start taking care of themselves, and to care less what others think. If we do not assist people to develop a healthy sense of identity we invite the negative aspects of the self-development ethic to come to the fore.

The new character has three negative traits. The first is an other-directed marketing orientation to life. People tend to trade their integrity for status and end up feeling alienated and detached. The second negative trait is an undisciplined self-indulgence that is rationalized as self-fulfillment. Finally, the self-development ethic may encourage getting as much as one can while giving as little as possible. This style is rationalized in terms of rights and entitlements. It is important to remember that these traits appear when men and women have no firm identity on which to build their self-esteem.

When religious professionals who are struggling with their personal and institutional identities feel they are being placed second to institutional needs, they will often resort to an egoistic solution. They try to protect what little self-esteem they have left by letting authority know that they will take care of themselves first. Thus, although the new self-development ethic appears less egocentric and narcissistic than past social characters, it is not necessarily less egoistic.

Outcomes of the self-development ethic

The self-development ethic has given rise to several important consequences in priestly, religious, and Church life. First, sisters, brothers, and priests have entered the age of psychology. For them, the importance of roles has diminished; a strong emphasis on relationships has developed; and interpersonalism in ministry and community has increased. Religious professionals avail themselves of psychotherapy more often, speak about self-determination, and act assertively. They defer to socal formality only when human concerns are not pressing. In other words, they are no longer willing to conform to the expectations of others with the hope of winning their approval.

In addition, religious professionals have a reduced sense of social integration. Organizations, roles, and norms previously associated with their lives have lost some of their power to provide meaning, identity, and satisfaction.

Finally, there is an increased search for intimacy among Church ministers, especially among men. The current popularity of priest support groups reflects this phenomenon. Many religious and priests, however, are neophytes when it comes to dealing with their interpersonal lives. Considerable educational work needs to be done in this area.

In brief, a new self-development social character is now emerging. Its impact on Church, religious, and priestly life is widespread and profound. Relationships, intimacy, and inter-personalism in ministry and life-style have taken on new importance. At the same time, many religious professionals feel less a part of their groups or Church society. They are unwilling to support institutional commitments at the expense of emotional development. Self-developing priests and religious expect authority to be rational, relational, and consultative in the decision-making process. These situations are normal in a transitional age. What about Church leaders in such a time of crisis?

The transitional Church leader in an age of self-development

In the past, forms of Church authority were adapted from secular models. As a consequence, they were cast in hierarchical, authoritarian, and power-based structures. Traditional notions of authority stressed the divinely instituted power of superiors which enabled them to command obedience and submission. Power was invested in the pope by reason of his office and by way of divine institution.

Today's Church leaders face an entirely different situation.[9] To lead well, they need to find, promote, and call forth the best aspects of their group's social character. The transitional nature of the age, however, makes their work doubly difficult. They must seek out, encourage, and evoke not only the best qualities of the newly emerging social character but also those of the group's coexisting older one. In carrying out their task, something of a balancing act, leaders face many practical problems. In various parishes and religious communities, the exercise of leadership has been transformed into a power struggle. Some religious deny authority any claim over them. This situation may be a reflection of the negative side of the new self-development ethic. When people feel worthless and powerless, they will refuse to yield to authority. Convinced that authority cares little about them, these men and women fear a loss of their identity. As a consequence, they decide to look out for themselves. To deal

---

9. For additional discussions of leadership, see entire issue of "Crisis of Leadership," *Humanitas* 14, no. 1 (November 1978) and *New Catholic World* 223, no. 1337 (September/October 1980).

with this situation, Christian leaders need patience and a capacity for human relationships. They must be willing to tolerate the individuality and autonomy of others. An additional tension is set up by those more rooted in an older ethic, who continue to look to authority for answers and decisions.

In addition, leaders need to understand their community's phase of development when determining the type of leadership they should provide. Four possible phases can be discerned in the history of Church communities: birth; expansion; peace and prosperity; crisis. The expectations of leadership are different during each phase.

In the first phase, the leader rallies the unformed group into a community with its own identity, meaning, and purpose. To allow this development, members give the leader authority over themselves. During the community's second and third phases structures and processes that express its identity are established. Laws and decrees are promulgated; the leader is now governor and ruler. The fourth phase, crisis and transition, is similar to the time when the community was called into existence. Something new but not yet visible is needed. During these times of transition, the community's identity is often threatened, though not its existence. As the character of the group changes, two forces rise up to confront the leader. The first demands that the community be kept as it was before any threat or crisis appeared. The second calls for leaders to guide the community through the transitional wilderness into a new promised land. This second task is the challenge of transitional leadership: to be both a mentor and a prophet.

Mentors are both parents and peers. Their relationships with others are not defined by roles but by the character and function of the relationships. Transitional Church leaders face three challenging tasks within their groups: to support and facilitate the realization of personal and institutional visions by mentoring; to serve as models for their members; and to guide and educate them by setting out a prophetic vision.

In facing their first task, transitional leaders capture and teach the gospel spirit as it is understood in today's world. Leaders of religious congregations and orders also assist members in re-working the individual and institutional dreams embodied in the founding charism and early life of the community. Institutional trappings are dropped and the original spirit reclaimed.

Second, transitional leaders undertake major efforts toward personal, spiritual, psychological, and institutional renewal. In this work they must allow for a period of exploration necessary for the purification that is part of these efforts. To complete this task leaders need to develop an understanding of the Church's historical and sociological development. They should also take their own personal, spiritual, and psychological growth seri-ously. In other words, today's Church leaders need a sense of history, tradition, and organizational change, an understanding of their own adult development, and a personal experience of God. They need all three; an understanding of sociology, Church politics, or group dynamics will be of little use without a rich spiritual life. The reverse is also true.

Finally, today's Church needs prophetic education not only for its leaders but also for those who are led. Effective leadership is necessary at all levels of the organization: local, regional, and national. Leaders need to take time to create a vision for their group. They fail to do this and undermine effective local leader-ship when they do not set limits with their leadership style. They spread themselves too thin, wasting their effectiveness. This fail-ure to define their roles and responsibilities and to adhere to these descriptions has serious results. Many Church leaders are little more than crisis managers. Provincial superiors who spend their energies in developing personal relationships with the 250 members of their province are not exercising the mentoring aspect of transitional leadership and are leaving themselves with little time or inclination to develop the prophetic aspects of their role. Failing to create a prophetic vision, they miss the oppor-tunity to call forth the best traits in the character of their group or to help its members chart a direction. Instead, they bring out the worst traits of some group members by fostering the fantasy that the provincial superior, or bishop, if that is the case, should be the all-caring and ever-attentive "mother" or "father" for whom they long. In addition, superiors who lead in this manner allow members to avoid dealing with their local leadership or primary group. Hence, unrealistic expectations of leadership continue to go unchallenged. In failing to undertake the educational work needed in this area, leaders seriously jeopardize the prophetic and mentoring aspects of their role. This is a critical loss for the new self-development ethic in today's transitional Church.

Conclusion

Today's religious professional leaders must be strong in the Spirit. They need a greater than average ability to read, persuade, and teach others. Abundant energy, patience, and hope are also necessary. To respond to the diverse needs of their groups' coexisting social characters, they must develop a sense of the future, a prophetic vision of what is anticipated but not yet seen. Making their own journeys of personal and spiritual transition and having a knowledge of the history and sociology of institutional change, these men and women are better able to guide others. They have seen the promised land as in a glass darkly and are willing to lead others toward it. However, today's Church leaders are beginning to realize that because of the transitional nature of the age their task of guiding others will take more time and energy than they had at first imagined. Like Moses, they themselves may never enter the "promised land" of the new beginning, the transition's third phase.

I would like to close this section with a word of encouragement to contemporary religious professionals discouraged by the pace and quality of renewal efforts. On my bookshelf rests a slim volume of essays by Francis Sweeney, a Jesuit priest, who spent over thirty years teaching English to Boston College freshmen. The title of his book captures some of the costs of change. It also suggests the time required to accomplish renewal. Sweeney entitled his essays "It will take a lifetime. . . ." For the successful completion of our present Church transition, I would add ". . . and then some."

In the midst of tumult, transition, and changing social characters, religious professionals are also being challenged by the alternating stable and transitional periods in their adult life. The nature of the present age introduces additional stress into the lives of priests and religious. What sort of developmental challenges do they face during their adult years in this time of transition? To answer this question, we need to look at the eras of the life cycle and the work of novice, middle, and later adulthood.

Part II: Change and Adult Maturity

Chapter Four

Novice adulthood:
Its choices and consequences

"Life is too big for us in the end," Rabbit Angstrom muses grimly, "what a threadbare thing we make of it."[1] As a young high-school basketball star, Rabbit shone brightly in his small Pennsylvania suburb of Mount Judge. Living for the present moment, he thought little of consequences. Now, at midlife, he makes some sober assessments. Faced with the consequences of earlier decisions, other middle-aged men and women also evaluate the meaning of their life. The conclusion they arrive at is somewhat different from Rabbit's. For them, life is a strange gift, one they often do not know how to use. It is, though, the only gift they have and they know it is a good one.

In recent years, interest in the life cycle has grown rapidly. Having had their fill of childhood and adolescent psychology,

---

1. Updike, *Rabbit is Rich,* p. 431. See also Updike's *Rabbit Run* (New York: Knopf, 1960) and *Rabbit Redux* (New York: Knopf, 1971). These three books trace Rabbit Angstrom's life from his late twenties through his midforties.

more people are asking: Is there life *after* youth? Do people change and grow following adolescence? Are there developmental rules that apply to everyone?

Initial reports about the adult years are encouraging. For example, people continue to develop even after having "grown up." Adulthood is a more exciting country than the land of childhood and adolescence. Although some uniformity exists among the life journeys of many adults, considerable variety is also evident. On the one hand, no one set of developmental rules applies to everyone. Some differences exist, for instance, between men and women.[2] Sociocultural and historical circumstances as well as life choices and commitments also affect people's development.

On the other hand, some principles apply across sex, historical circumstances, roles, and world view. Stable periods and times of change, for example, are found in every person's life. Relationships are of concern to men and women, teachers and housepainters, physicians and homemakers. The search for life's meaning is everyone's challenge.

In this chapter I will examine the conventional wisdom about adulthood and discuss the first several years of that journey, focusing on the eras and the stable and transitional periods of the life cycle. Finally, I will trace the religious professional's journey through the years of early adulthood.

Conventional wisdom about the adult years

Conventional wisdom maintains that children grow and develop, whereas adults only age. For many years educational institutions and social scientists maintained this myth. Consider a trip to your local library. An impressive number of texts and monographs examining childhood and adolescence will reward any search for books about developmental psychology. Works devoted to adulthood, however, will be few and far between.

Until recently, growth observed during the adult years was judged to be erratic and unpredictable. For example, men and

---

2. See Carol Gilligan, *In a Different Voice* (Cambridge: Harvard University Press, 1982).

women with courage enough to talk about their questions and struggles were dismissed as "middlescents." Worse yet, they were told their struggles were symptomatic of a failure to address developmental tasks at a more appropriate age, that is, during childhood and adolescence. According to this strange view of human development people, like cars, are put together in the assembly plant of childhood. Road tested during adolescence, they pass inspection as finished products at about age eighteen. Any change after that is considered a malfunction.

The life experience of men and women contradicts this stagnant view of human development. Too many people are testifying that more dramatic change has taken place in their lives *after* the adolescent years than before. In the past, people's fear of rejection stopped them from sharing these changes. They hid the guilt, confusion, exhilaration, anger, emptiness, and periodic depression that accompanied their growth. The lack of a common frame of reference or even a language with which to examine and describe adult development hindered free exchange about the challenge of maturity.

The task of developing a framework is difficult. The following story from Idries Shah's *Tales of the Dervishes* illustrates the dilemmas involved.[3] Only blind men lived in a city behind Gohr. When a king and his army arrived and camped near the city, they brought an elephant with them. The town's inhabitants were awed by tales of this creature. Wanting to learn more about it, they rushed out of the town in search of the elephant. The blind men were forced to get their information by touching the animal. One man reported to his fellow citizens that the elephant was a "large rough thing, wide and broad like a rug." Another, having felt its trunk, insisted that the creature was rather, "like a straight and hollow pipe, awful and destructive." Each person's understanding was incomplete and inaccurate. A number of the elephant's characteristics needed to be explored before any of the blind men could give an accurate composite description of it.

---

3. Idries Shah, *Tales of the Dervishes* (New York: E. P. Dutton, 1970), pp. 25-26.

One can avoid a similar error in defining what it means to be an adult by examining many different aspects of the adult years. A look at the seasons of the life cycle and events shaping them is a good place to begin this task.

Forces shaping the life cycle

Nature gives us several clues about the adult life cycle. The year has four seasons and each has unique characteristics. Spring blossoms follow winter's desolation; summer's warmth is remembered long after autumn's leaves change color, the days grow shorter, and the year begins to die. A person's life moves through seasons similar to those found in nature. There are times of new beginning filled with springtime excitement; endings and leave-takings marked by loss and a sense of autumnal death. Feelings of well-being are associated with the summertime of life, while bleakness and despair can take on the character of one's personal New England winter.

A number of forces and circumstances shape people's lives. For example, particular historical events have an impact. Consider men and women who grew up during the Great Depression. It shaped their sense of security, manner of saving, and concerns around money. What about people who were college students at the time of the Vietnam War? Did this experience affect their trust of government? Probably. Vatican II was a significant influence for many priests and religious. For some, it resulted in a new self-understanding and appreciation of their life-style. Others were left confused, angry, and uncertain about the meaning of their life commitment.

People are also affected by their particular sociocultural world, family, ethnic group, race, religion, socioeconomic class, even political party. For example, the success of recent dramatic presentations like *Mass Appeal* and *Sister Mary Ignatius Explains It All for You* is an example of the public's interest in "growing up Catholic."[4] Foods and customs differ among

---

4. *Mass Appeal* and *Sister Mary Ignatius Explains It All for You* are two current dramas. The first tells the story of the relationship between a young, idealistic, newly ordained priest and a rather crusty old pastor. The second is a parody of Catholic education during the 1950s.

Irish, Italian, and Jewish families. The struggles of black Americans during the past two decades point out how race can influence people's view of their world.

Finally, various roles shape men's and women's lives. They may be parents, friends, religious sisters, brothers or priests, school or hospital administrators, lovers, or members of various groups and organizations. Each circumstance shaping their lives, each role they assume during their lifetime, allows them to live out various parts of themselves. Some circumstances and roles are central. They resist change. Others are peripheral and can be dispensed with more easily. On the one hand, for example, the role of parent is not given up lightly. Neither do most people change a life commitment without serious thought and emotional upheaval. On the other hand, a number of people can change residences, acquaintances, and some group memberships without undue stress.

Historical events, roles, and one's sociocultural world can also be a drawback. They may inhibit the development of an individual's personality. No one way of living in the world allows people to live out all their values, dreams, and potential roles and personality characteristics. In making choices and living out particular roles, men and women must necessarily neglect other aspects of their personality. As a result, they need to change their life structure periodically. This change allows some neglected, inhibited parts of themselves to be lived out. Times of life transition provide the means for this necessary change in life structure.

Periods of stability and transition

A person's life structure does not change capriciously or suddenly, nor does it remain static. Instead, it appears to evolve through a series of alternating periods of stability and transition. The stable periods last six to seven years; the transitional, four to five years each.[5]

Each stable and each transitional period has its own distinct tasks reflecting its place in the life cycle. For example, many

---

5. See Levinson, *Seasons of a Man's Life*, pp. 49-56.

priests experience a transition around age thirty.[6] It is strongly colored by their need to fashion a life for themselves, one in which they can realize their youthful dreams and values. In contrast, during their transition at midlife these men face different challenges: the loss of youth, a senior position in ministry, inner tensions that must be reworked.

Every stable period has three characteristic aspects. At its outset, people make some type of life decision. Next, they attempt to build a life structure around this decision. Finally, they strive to attain their goals and values within this structure. Imagine a young woman who develops an interest in religious life. What might she do? Today, she would probably first investigate a variety of communities and learn about their spirit, life-style, and apostolic work. At the same time, she would determine whether she had the necessary education and other prerequisites for entering communities of interest to her. Eventually, this woman makes a decision, applies to a particular group, completes the necessary tasks for admission, and begins her formation within the community. During her formative years, and later, she works to attain her particular goals and values within the group. Another young woman decides to be an attorney. She goes through a similar process of investigation, choice, and the building of a life structure. Although some change occurs during a stable period, one's basic life structure remains fixed. Stable periods, though, are not stagnant ones! Rather, growing and feeling purposeful, people set their sights on the future. Transitional periods are somewhat different.

Most life transitions are times for second thoughts, when people's sights are set on the past rather than the future. They question their life structure and the direction it has taken. A middle-aged priest, for example, feels lonely, confused, and dissatisfied. He has doubts about his commitments. As this man evaluates his

---

6. See Sean D. Sammon, "Relationship between Life Stress, Level of Ego Identity, and Age of Commitment to Central Life Structure Components in Age Thirty Transition Catholic Religious Professional Men" (Ph.D. diss., Fordham University, 1982).

life, he wonders whether a change would bring back some of his previous enthusiasm.

Transitions usually begin with an ending. A lengthy period follows when people feel stranded and "up in the air." Finally, there is a new beginning. During a life transition, most people face this twofold developmental challenge: terminate the existing life structure; work toward building a new one. To overcome it, people have to reappraise what has gone before in their lives and explore various possibilities for change in themselves and their world. In completing this work, they form the basis for a new life structure to serve them during the next stable period. A transitional period ends when questioning and exploring have lost their urgency, and building, living within, and enhancing the new life structure begin.

Jack Coleman did his transitional work well.[7] During a two-month sabbatical, this former Haverford College president worked as a garbage collector, ditch digger, and sandwich-and-salad man in a Boston restaurant. Upon returning to his incredulous college faculty, Coleman faced some rather pointed questions about his sanity. After all, his sabbatical report was not what was expected from a college president! How did he explain his behavior? For years, he told his faculty, students had come to him with this question: what is the meaning of my life and does college play a role in it? Coleman had invariably advised them to do something different with their life—to take a job and spend time with people whose experience was not their own. Eventually, they would examine their values against those of others and make a decision about their life. Coleman took his own advice seriously and had no regrets. He later used the knowledge gained during his sabbatical when he became president of a foundation and reshaped its field of activity to include some blue-collar projects.

To benefit from life transitions, it is important to recall several facts about them. First of all, they take time. A person's characteristic way of dealing with endings also has an effect.

---

7. See John R. Coleman, *Blue Collar Journal: A College President's Sabbatical* (Philadelphia: J. B. Lippincott, 1974).

However, regardless of individual differences, transitional times cause people to reevaluate their relationships, life commitments, ministry, and aspects of their personality and world. In undertaking transitional tasks, men and women discover that their previous life structure is inadequate for the challenges they now face. As a result, they need to be willing to change some commitments or rework old ones. A loss of roles and feelings of disengagement, disenchantment, and disorientation are common. Painful as they may be, transitional periods help people move from one era of the life cycle to the next. Stated simply, every transition is an end and a beginning, a death and a birth, a departure and an arrival.[8]

Eras of the life cycle

The life cycle can be divided into five distinct but overlapping eras.[9] Each lasts approximately twenty-five years and has characteristic features. *Pre-adulthood* spans the years from birth until the early twenties. *Early adulthood* gets under way around age eighteen or nineteen and continues through the early forties. *Middle adulthood* comes next. Initiated by the midlife transition, this era generally begins during one's late thirties and comes to a close about the time of retirement, age sixty-five for many people. Men and women between sixty and eighty-five are living their *late adulthood.* *Late, late adulthood* rewards those who in the words of Psalm 90 "have life lasting for eighty years or more with good health."

The fundamental changing character of people's lives moves them from one era to another. Consider a religious sister who is a teacher. Moving into her early sixties, she looks forward to a reduced teaching load. She also looks back on her life and assesses its meaning. This woman feels "old" for the first time in her life, and she is surprised that others also see her this way. Finally, knowing that she has already lived more years than the

---

8. See Levinson, *Seasons of a Man's Life,* pp. 49-56.

9. Ibid., pp. 18-39; see also Wendy Ann Stewart, "A Psychosocial Study of the Formation of the Early Adult Life Structure in Women" (Ph.D. diss., Columbia University, 1977).

number that lie ahead for her, this sister wonders what her life would have been like if she had made other choices, finalized other commitments, lived another life. Over the course of a few years she will make changes as she moves from middle to late adulthood.

Early adulthood

Early adulthood, which gets under way during a person's late teens, begins with a transition. The ages seventeen through twenty-two witness a number of changes. Most seventeen-year-olds, for example, have several things on their mind, one of the preeminent ones being: how can I get away from home and out on my own? Today, America supports one of history's largest socially sanctioned escapes from the home. College! These years are a time of exploration and great physical and psychological energy. They are also among the most stressful and unstable of adult life. People separate from home, begin to change the balance of dependence and independence in their relationships, relate to adults more as peers, and think of themselves as "growing up." In doing so, they make some initial choices for adult living, consolidate their identity, and begin to fashion their life's Dream.

The Dream

One's Dream is an important motivating influence throughout life.[10] Often a vague vision at first, it begins as an answer to this question: what am I going to do with my adult life? Whatever its nature, people face the crucial challenge of whether and how to put the Dream into effect in their life. Building a life around their Dream, men and women enhance their chance for fulfillment. Those who betray their Dream or are unable to pursue it face later consequences. A young man, for example, may struggle with two possible life directions: one that expresses his Dream, another that does not. He can move in the first life

---

10. See Levinson, *Seasons of a Man's Life,* pp. 91-97; and Sammon, "Age Thirty Catholic Religious Professional Men," pp. 9-11.

direction or can be pushed away from his Dream by parents, external factors such as money, aspects of his personality, or a special talent. People who betray their Dream often succeed in life. Having lost touch with the Dream, however, their motivation and sense of purpose die.

In attempting to build a life around their Dream, some men and women take advantage of a "psychosocial moratorium." A period of experimentation during which people delay their life commitments, this moratorium allows them to experiment with various roles and ways of living out their life. As a result, they clarify their Dream and find a place in society that seems made uniquely for them.

Identity

Late adolescent men and women also need to form an initial adult identity. [11] This term refers to the feeling of knowing who you are and where your life is going. Identity is not purchased cheaply. To achieve one, people must be willing to do three things: explore options for living; experience crises; and make a commitment.

Commitment describes people's personal investment in what they have chosen. In contrast, crisis refers to a period of struggle and questioning during which people rethink old roles and life plans. They also test out some new ones. Most adolescents find themselves in this situation. A number of them experiment in fantasy with a variety of careers and relationships. For example, on Monday a fifteen-year-old boy plans to be a physicist; by Thursday medicine is more attractive. Adolescent love relationships are often short-lived and turbulent.

Many young men and women in formation for religious and priestly life also experience crises. How many novices think about withdrawing from the novitiate? At times, almost any other life direction is more attractive than the one they have chosen. Other young professed religious and newly ordained

---

11. See Sammon, "Age Thirty Catholic Religious Professional Men," pp. 19-37, as well as discussion about the relationship between identity and commitment age.

priests fall in love. They wonder seriously whether to pursue a committed relationship instead of their present life choice. Whenever people begin to explore other options for living, they experience crisis. Whatever they decide, their struggle helps them form an identity. Young men and women struggle with options in many of these areas: life direction, career choice, relationships, sexuality, and separation from home. Those who face the challenge head-on eventually establish their place in the world.

Some persons skip the exploration and crisis stages. By jumping to commitment, they foreclose their identity. The results are disappointing. The situation is similar to ordering a suit through the mail—it seldom fits properly! The shoulders are always a little too wide, the jacket too tight. The same thing happens with a foreclosed identity. Not being tailor-made for the person, it looks as though it belongs to someone else.

People who foreclose their identity commit themselves too early. They fail to explore their options for living. Refusing to question their values and goals, these men and women commit themselves because of external circumstances or to please authority. This is a dangerous decision, and later in life it exacts a cost.

What do people who foreclose their identity look like? Usually they appear stable, sober, and responsible. However, they also lack curiosity and independence. Repression is their major defense. Having foreclosed indentity, they generally endorse the authoritarian values of obedience, strong leadership, and respect for authority. They are somewhat passive and maintain strong ties with their parents' outlook and standards. Their relationships with others are often stereotyped. Rather than relating as a person, they are more comfortable with a role.

Identity throughout the life cycle

Although first appearing during early adulthood's onset, identity crises also occur during any life transition. At these times, people reevaluate their previous commitments, explore alternative ways of living, and move toward building a life structure to serve them during the ensuing stable period. Updike's character Tom Marshfield, for example, begins his transitional period and search for a new identity with this question: "Who am I?" Seeing his face in the mirror he says, "I do not recognize it as mine. It no more fits my inner light than the shade of a bridge lamp fits its bulb."[12]

During early adulthood, people wonder who they are becoming. Later on in life they question who they have become. A middle-aged religious sister, for example, develops a relationship with a man. With time they grow closer, the bond deepens. She imagines what it would be like to spend her life with this man. The relationship introduces her to aspects of herself of which she was not aware. Former obligations and present commitments come under close scrutiny. She has many feelings: wonder, deep affection, confusion, loss, fear, guilt, and fulfillment. She also experiences a loss of her old identity, and former ways of understanding herself no longer make sense. For a period of time her life is in turmoil as she attempts to meet community obligations and maintain this important relationship. Eventually, she decides to remain within her community. She finds, though, that she is a new person. The process has been painful, but outlooks have been transformed, needs recognized, the preciousness of her life confirmed. Her journey in this relationship has given rise to a new and more genuine identity.

This woman had achieved an initial identity earlier in her life. She still, however, experienced crisis when faced with a transition. The crisis territory was familiar, though, for she had explored it at other times (other stages of development). Thus she was able to deal with it successfully again.

The prognosis is less favorable for men and women who previously foreclosed their identity. During any transition, they are highly vulnerable to an identity crisis. They defend themselves by demanding that their environment remain constant and consistently supportive. Lacking such an environment, they are thrown into distress. Panic and intense self-questioning ensue.

---

12. John Updike, *A Month of Sundays* (New York: Fawcett, 1975), p. 7.

For some people who foreclosed previously, this experience helps them achieve a new identity. Others, however, shed one foreclosed identity only to take up another hastily.

Many men and women entered religious and priestly life in their late teens. They gave themselves little opportunity to explore. Does this fact suggest they also foreclosed their identity? Not necessarily. Identity does not appear to be related to age of commitment; rather, it is one's life experiences that are important. Some people enter priesthood or religious community late in life and still have a foreclosed identity. The essential ingredients for identity are exploration, crisis, and commitment. If the first two are missing at any age, the risk of foreclosing identity is high. A genuine identity assists people to enter society with confidence and to assume their adult responsibilities.

The novice years of early adulthood

The period from the late teen years through the midthirties, novice adulthood, is a genuine novitiate experience during which men and women prepare to enter the adult world. In a religious novitiate, novices learn the history of the community, continue to develop an intense prayer life, and are schooled in the ascetical and spiritual life. At the end of this experience, they make their first public commitment to the group they wish to join. In one sense, these first vows make them "card-carrying members" of the group. No longer do they feel they are impersonating a sister, brother, or priest.

Novice adulthood is similar. Many men and women in their twenties fear they are impersonating an adult. A young man, for example, is ordained at twenty-six. Three weeks later he is counseling a middle-aged couple with a marital difficulty. Feeling like their son, he wonders what in heaven's name he will be able to do for these people. Consider also the young teacher. She worries about being mistaken for a student aide at the first parent-teachers meeting. Feeling insecure as an adult, she fears being unmasked at any moment. Around their midthirties, most people lose this sense of insecurity. Having faced the developmental tasks of the period, they feel more at home being an adult.

Novice adulthood has three distinct parts: a stable period enclosed by two periods of transition. A number of religious professionals entered initial formation just as their novice adulthood was getting under way. As they began novitiate or seminary education, these men and women also started a period of transition, their early adult transition. Many candidates looked forward to testing out their vocation. They were asking: "Is this really the life for me?" Instead, many found formation environments where exploration was discouraged or treated as a temptation. If carried out at all, experimentation had to be quiet, internal, or secret.

At many seminaries and novitiates, life was highly structured. Candidates lived by the bell, and their daily schedule was clearly delineated. Customs like early rising, great silence, warnings about "particular friendships," prayers in common, conferences with the rector, and a number of other previously foreign activities soon became second nature. In these environments, many priests, sisters, and brothers grew intellectually. Their emotional and psychological development, however, was often arrested. Some of them failed to move from the world of childhood and adolescence into adulthood. They did not really separate from home. Values and goals were not questioned, and parental outlooks and standards were adopted unsynthesized. Others avoided exploring relationships and alternative options for living out their life. The structure and restrictions of religious formation notwithstanding, still others managed to struggle with issues of growth. They formed relationships, questioned their vocational choice, worked to develop a genuine spiritual life, and began to discover new and exciting aspects of their personality. In doing so, some also questioned whether the philosophy and rules of seminary and novitiate formation were more of a hindrance than an aid to developing a healthy religious and priestly life.

In summary, during the transition into early adulthood, a time of exploration and testing of possibilities, a large number of religious professionals were living in highly restricted and structured formation environments. This situation gave rise to important consequences several years later.

Becoming part of the adult world

Most people in their twenties are not ready to make enduring *inner* commitments. Instead they continue a pattern of exploration and commitment. Difficult as it is to balance these two activities, most people choose one of four approaches. Taking one approach, some men and women fall on the side of commitment. Their key choices regarding life direction and relationships are made during their transition into early adulthood. In making strong commitments at the outset of their twenties, these people hope to build a life structure that will endure. Many religious professionals are included among these early committers. They pronounced first vows during their early twenties or were ordained a few years later. As their adolescent years came to a close, these men and women were well immersed in a religious life-style.

Those people who move tentatively through their twenties exemplify a second approach to the challenge of exploration and commitment. They lead transient lives. Their jobs may change; relationships come and go; places of residence vary. These men and women often fail to invest much of themselves in their world or allow their world to influence them. Rather than living life, they drift through it.

Still others choose stability in one part of their life, transiency in another. For example, a man in this category may commit himself to a religious life-style but also continue to explore various options for ministry. A woman who focuses her energy on a career and explores a number of relationships also illustrates this approach.

Finally, those taking a fourth approach lead nomadic lives and remain uncommitted during their early twenties. About age twenty-five or twenty-six, they begin to form a more stable life. Today, a number of men and women seeking admission to religious life fall into this fourth category. Having spent their early twenties exploring, they become more serious about their life as they move toward thirty. They feel an increasing need to settle down and do something constructive with their life.

Having made an early commitment, many brothers, sisters, and priests experience a stable period during their twenties. Feeling appreciated, they are enthusiastic about their ministry. Relationships and life projects are a challenge. Hardly a time of stagnation, stability and hope for the future mark these years.

Although some life structures are more satisfying than others, no structure is without flaws and contradictions. Regardless of the choices people make during their twenties, they stumble across an important growth-inducing lesson as they approach thirty: all choices made in life have consequences. Many men and women regret some earlier life choices. They convince themselves that in making some other choices they would have escaped suffering any consequences. This is simply not possible. Different choices made give rise to other consequences. For example, a young man who commits himself to religious life during his early twenties often comes to age thirty and wonders if he made his life decisions too early. He questions: "Did I explore enough? Did I really know what I was getting into?" This man imagines that if he had spent his twenties exploring he would have avoided all his present pain and questioning. He needs only to meet another man who did just that to learn the error of his thinking. "Explorers" come to their late twenties and see others as settled and doing something with their life. Wondering what is wrong with them, they feel an increased need to settle down and give purpose to their own life. No one escapes the consequences of their life decisions. One of human development's great paradoxes is this: people are required to make crucial life choices before they have the knowledge, judgment, and self-understanding to choose wisely. If they put off these choices until they feel truly ready, however, the delay may exact a greater price.[13]

Transition at age thirty

About the end of one's twenties, a significant transition gets under way. Life has become more restrictive and serious, and people need an opportunity to work on the flaws and limitations

13. See Levinson, *Seasons of a Man's Life.*

of their life structure in order to initiate a new one for completing early adulthood. With the novelty of adulthood wearing off, many young people as they pass thirty have serious questions and doubts about forming a life structure worth having.[14] At this time, men and women also have second thoughts about their earlier life choices. They wonder if some changes are necessary. Realizing that their commitments cannot be lived out in quite the same way as just a few years ago, these men and women start to rework or alter them. During this period people question many aspects of their life. They ask themselves: "What am I doing with my life? What do I truly want for myself and others? Do I really care about anybody else? What have I done with my early Dream?" Stress and self-examination mark the transition. One Church minister put it this way:

> I seem to be at a difficult age. Much of what were real values for me and gave real meaning to my life has changed or disappeared. Perhaps those things which I thought were goals, such as being a good teacher or fitting into my religious community, were only part of a wider goal, but right now I'm not sure what that is. [I'm also] questioning my religious vocation now moreso [sic] than ever. The realization of the life commitment I have made is a sudden reality.[15]

The transition around age thirty leads to changes in internal commitments and the structure of one's life. People may differ in the kinds of changes they make, but at the end of the period life is always different from what it was at the outset. There are several reasons for this. To begin with, unresolved adolescent conflicts often reappear during the transition. One has another

---

14. Ibid.

15. Sammon, "Age Thirty Catholic Religious Professional Men," p. 99. This study investigated the age-thirty transition among religious professional men. A similar investigation of women is planned. Although Levinson's work has also been primarily with men, he is completing a major study examining the adult development of women. See also Sheila Murphy's excellent study of midlife religious women, *Midlife Wanderer: The Woman Religious in Midlife Transition* (Whitinsville, Mass.: Affirmation Books, forthcoming).

chance to work on them and come to more satisfying resolutions. For example, a young man may have avoided dealing with his sexual identity during his teen years. In his early thirties, he finds himself troubled anew by questions about his sexual identity. By facing these questions, this man can grow to understand, accept, and integrate his sexuality into his life. Other men in their twenties discover that they are not ready to form a sexually free and loving relationship with another person. They feel insecure, have questions about their attractiveness as people, and are unable to take those risks necessary for an intimate relationship of equality. By struggling with the developmental tasks of their twenties and thirties, around midlife many are able to form relationships through which they can grow and be transformed.

Many other changes also occur at about age thirty. People alter their life structure. Such necessary work allows men and women to commit themselves to the crucial choices that form the structure for their immediate future. Two Church ministers in their early thirties summarized their developmental challenges in this way:

> I used to think [that the structure of my life] was crystal clear. Now I am less sure. I feel as though I am growing and discovering who I am apart from a professional or religious role. It is important for me at this stage of my life to have an identity apart from work or role.
>
> At times, though, I feel like an eighteen-year-old again. I'm beginning to ask at thirty the same questions I asked back then: "Who am I? Am I sure this is the life for me?"[16]

Around the age of thirty many religious and priests experience an increase in their level of stress. Several events can lead to their discomfort. Some people find that gaining new members within the community is enough to cause difficulty. Others are distressed to discover that their understanding of their religious vows and the practical living out of them begin to change. Still others begin a love relationship; have a friend leave religious life; experience changes in ministry; discover new aspects of

16. Sammon, "Age Thirty Catholic Religious Professional Men," p. 99.

their sexuality; experience the death of a parent or other close family member; or have an outstanding personal achievement. Even when their life change is a positive one, men and women still experience stress because they must adjust to new understandings, feelings, and demands. In struggling to adapt to their changed life situation, people experience the confusion and upheaval that can lead to self-discovery and personal, emotional, and spiritual development.

Novice adulthood's developmental tasks

The transition around age thirty provides priests and men and women religious with an opportunity to reassess their lives. They examine the consequences of their commitments or lack of them. The period also serves this purpose: people take time out to evaluate their work on the developmental tasks of novice adulthood; that is, forming a Dream, mentor relationships, a ministry, and relationships of intimacy.[17] Here again, there is both bad and good news. First, the bad news. These tasks are important and need to be addressed. The good news? By age thirty, some work on even a few of them is all that can be expected.

Forming and beginning to live out one's Dream is an important task of novice adulthood. At about age thirty, men and women judge their success in this area. They examine their lifestyle, commitments, relationships, and future directions in the light of their Dream. Some people find that minor adjustments are necessary to bring their life into line with their early Dream. In making them, they free themselves of the adolescent tyranny that is part of any early Dream. For example, a woman religious cannot be a sister at thirty in the same way she imagined she would be at eighteen. Her earlier commitment must be questioned and reworked. To keep the spirit of her Dream and realize

---

17. See Levinson, *Seasons of a Man's Life,* pp. 90-111. Again, though Levinson has been working with men, many religious women have indicated that past formation and life-style structures may have influenced their development along the lines that Levinson alludes to in his work with men.

its relevance for her life today, she makes adjustments in her life-style, relationships, and life direction.

Other people discover they have betrayed their early Dream. Trapped and feeling aimless, their early hopes appear dashed. These men and women also face a challenge: to bring their life into line with the spirit of their early Dream.

Mentoring relationships are an important part of novice adulthood. They nurture the Dream of the novice adult and facilitate its implementation. Mentors are both parents and peers, not solely one or the other. They are psychological mothers and fathers. In times of stress, they provide the novice adult with counsel and support. They can also serve as models by their own achievements and way of life. As the mentoring relationship evolves, novice adults gain a fuller sense of their own authority and capabilities.

This pattern is illustrated in the comments of a twenty-eight-year-old Church minister who sees his colleagues as mentors:

> By sharing my dreams, ideas, ambitions, successes and failures with them, [I learned] to see myself better and to clarify my ideals. As a result they have encouraged me in what I have chosen as a direction in my life.[18]

A number of religious professionals cite spiritual directors as important mentors. Others mention religious superiors and those men and women who initiated them into ministry and provided an example of a committed life-style. Mentoring is an important part of any healthy institution. The quality of life within a group can be judged, in part, by the quality of mentoring taking place. If it is poor, then group life will suffer.

Forming a ministry is a task that extends over the entire period of novice adulthood. Priests and religious approach this challenge in several different ways. For some, their ministry unfolds sequentially. A twenty-eight-year-old Church minister and educator had this experience:

---

18. Sammon, "Age Thirty Catholic Religious Professional Men," p. 101.

In the past six years I have been in [several] different situations. . . . Each situation had different demands and needed renewed creativity and provided [few] or no guidelines. Having felt frustration at times, I would say I was quite successful in what I did. I do have a better understanding of my capabilities and desires.[19]

Others form their ministry through crisis. They may lose a job or fail in a particular apostolate. A lengthy period of self-examination and struggle often follows as men and women try to regain self-confidence and discern the focus of their ministry. A third group of people find around age thirty that their ministry is in transition. A thirty-one-year-old teacher and religious brother captured this situation in these remarks:

I've been moderately successful in attempts to form a ministry within the last two years. I have moved from teaching mathematics to religious studies which interest me a great deal. My next step is to move into pastoral ministry or religious activities director for a school or parish. I am going for studies in this field. I hope within the next year or so to be working in this field.[20]

About age thirty some men and women find success but little satisfaction in their ministry. Others still in preparation for ministry are unsure of their future success or happiness. Still others fear the changes that may be required to bring their ministry more into line with their early Dream. Finally, a few credit their inability to form a satisfying ministry to outside circumstances. For example, one religious professional feeling considerable dissatisfaction with his present ministry said: "I have been moved around a great deal and have not been given the ability to succeed or remain in one spot."[21] Whatever pattern they exhibit, people ask a number of serious questions as they struggle to form a ministry during the novice years of early adulthood.

As men and women approach the end of their twenties, the question of relationships takes on greater import. Beginning to

---

19. Ibid., p. 102.
20. Ibid., p. 103.
21. Ibid.

feel more secure in ministry, they concentrate their attention on other aspects of their life. Some religious professionals fall in love for the first time. This experience of infatuation is an important step toward building loving adult relationships with other men and women. A healthy priestly and religious life includes caring relationships that grow over the years. Working together on projects and apostolates many young religious and priests find that care for another is awakened. With time, it begins to grow and deepen. Such growing relationships of love sometimes frighten others within the diocese or community. They move to limit the relationship, and express concern and disapproval. These reactions are often not very helpful. Men and women struggling to live a chaste life need to be able to love others in a passionate and human way. If they cannot, who will be attracted to join them? Few people want to live without love. Living with chaste men and women who can express affection spontaneously, be unguarded, and relax with others, people grow to be more themselves.

For those young religious who experience a deep loving relationship with another person during this stage of development, many feelings are involved: joy, jealousy, pain, preoccupation, disappointment, affection, anger, a rare tenderness. Men and women are transformed by such relationships. For some their religious and priestly life is deepened, their commitment grows stronger with the support of this loving relationship. Others, however, begin to question their earlier commitment. One young man summarized his concerns this way:

> Because of a deep relationship in my life with a woman I have come to realize the need in my life for intimacy. This has deepened my relationships with others. What I have to find out is if I can live a celibate life without the intense intimacy found only in marriage. It's a rather painful process, yet exciting in that I have found out aspects of myself of which I was unaware.[22]

Whatever the outcome of decisions made in a relationship, we need to support others as they search for the place of intimacy in

---

22. Ibid., p. 104.

their lives. Forming relationships of intimacy is an important developmental task for novice adults, one whose successful completion depends on a strong sense of identity. Intimacy means letting someone else close enough to me that I can possibly be changed by the relationship. If I am unsure of my sense of self, however, I will be reluctant to let anyone close. Although middle adulthood may present the best time for free and loving relationships to mature, many have their roots in novice adulthood.

Conclusion

For many religious professionals, the transition around age thirty is a time for second thoughts. Some of them, having made early commitments, now question the wisdom of their choices. They wonder if they have explored other life possibilities enough. Those who make later commitments also experience a transition. Life has become more serious and restrictive, and the pull to make deeper and more meaningful commitments is strong. For a large number of priests and men and women religious, these years are a time of change, upheaval, and growth. They examine their previous stable period, assess their success or failure at novice adulthood's challenging tasks, and decide what parts of their life must be given up or appreciably changed. Many wonder what is missing in their life. During this period a significant lesson is learned: all of life's choices have their consequences.

Near the end of the transition, religious professionals switch their focus away from internal developmental work and more toward their future. They may find a new life direction, strengthen their previous commitments, or, in some instances, make new choices. The chief task of novice adulthood is to find one's place in the world and to create a suitable, viable life structure. The age-thirty transition gives men and women a chance to reconsider earlier choices and to make changes, large or small, in themselves and their world. The life structure that emerges near the end of novice adulthood has tremendous implications for the future. For some people, it is flawed. Avoiding questions such as personal identity, intimacy, ministry, and the meaning of their life, some men and women form a structure that is neither suitable for themselves nor helpful for living in the world. Others, however, having struggled with the period's developmental tasks, move into their thirties and discover a productive time for ministry, enhanced personal relationships, developing spirituality, and hope for the future. Their thirties are years during which they look ahead and have a feeling of accomplishment in their work, a period of purposefulness and growth. It is also the period of relative calm that comes just prior to the major transition that gets under way near the end of one's thirties. Marking, for some, their entrance into the afternoon of life, it is aptly named the midlife transition.

Chapter Five

Midway through the journey

"When you've been through a death threatening experience," former Iran hostage Morehead Kennedy was quoted as saying, "you are suddenly confronted with your real self. Most of us go through life chasing after a person who never really exists: our *idea* of ourself." Elaborating on his observation, Kennedy recalled a psychiatrist's advice to the returned Americans: "Don't try to chase after an idealized self. Come to terms with the person you really are."[1] These remarks capture the developmental challenge that confronts midlife men and women: accepting one's eventual mortality and beginning the journey away from early adulthood's experimental quality and toward the inward focus of the middle years.[2] To accomplish this task, people evaluate the decisions, accomplishments, direction, and meaning of

1. See "Moorhead Kennedys: Building a Better Life," in the *New York Times,* May 11, 1981 (Nadine Brozan's interview with the Morehead Kennedys).

2. The following are but a few of the excellent summaries of research on the middle years now available: Janice Brewi and Anne Brennan, *Mid-Life: Psychological and Spiritual Perspectives* (New York: Crossroads, 1982); Calvin A. Colarusso and Robert A. Nemiroff, *Adult Development* (New York: Plenum, 1981), especially chaps. 7, 8, 9; Janet Zollinger Giele, ed., *Women in the Middle Years* (New York: Wiley and Sons, 1982); John G. Howells, ed., *Modern Perspectives in the Psychiatry of Middle Age* (New York: Brunner/Mazel, 1981); Levinson, *Seasons of a Man's Life*; Lillian B. Rubin, *Women of a Certain Age: The Midlife Search for Meaning* (New York: Harper and Row, 1979); and Evelyn Eaton Whitehead and James D. Whitehead, *Christian Life Patterns* (New York: Doubleday, 1979).

the past four or so decades of their life. They also reexamine early dreams and values. In doing so, some men and women begin to realize they have lived out their ideals. Others discover for the first time that they have omitted important aspirations from their life fabric. Oscar Wilde described the midlife developmental dilemma cogently: "The gods have two ways of dealing harshly with us: the first is to deny us our dreams, and the second is to grant them."

Recently, interest in the transition at midlife has grown rapidly. People are asking: What is this transition about? What are its characteristics? Is it a normal part of adulthood? What makes it different from other transitions? Can one survive it and find greater integrity and happiness in the middle and later years?

In this chapter I will address such questions about the middle years and their place in the life cycle by describing the characteristic features of the transition at midlife; demonstrating that the midlife transition is an invitation to a fuller interior life; and identifying and discussing the period's developmental tasks.

Midlife transition described

Dante said it well in *The Divine Comedy*: "In the middle of the journey of my life, I came to myself within a dark wood where the straight way was lost. Ah, how hard it is to tell of that wood, savage and harsh and dense. The thought of which renews my fear. So bitter is it that death is hardly more."[3] A number of commentators interpret Dante's words as an allegorical description of the gates of hell. Others disagree. They argue that the poet's statement is rather a reflection of his state of mind as he went into exile from his beloved native city. Still others suggest that Dante was reflecting on his own midlife transition. If that is the case, the poet's words indicate how high the stakes are at midlife.

This four-to-five-year period of evaluation and change begins around age forty. Early adulthood is dying. Middle adulthood is not yet born. The period between these two events—the midlife

---

3. Dante Alighieri, *The Divine Comedy,* trans. John Aitken Carlyle (New York: Random House, Vintage Books, 1950), p. 11.

transition—is important in the life of every man and woman for several reasons.

Facing mortality

During this time people face the actuality of their own eventual death. This is the core of the transition at midlife: the experience of one's mortality. Many young adults identify easily with the late William Saroyan's quip, "Everybody has got to die, but I believe that an exception will be made in my case." Although they readily admit that death will also happen to them, this eventuality is taken on faith.

At midlife, however, men and women join the ranks of those for whom death may soon be a personal experience. Three factors work together and convince them of this fact. First of all, parents, older relatives, colleagues, and friends are dying. This "buffer generation" that, thus far, protected them from death is beginning to thin out. During early adulthood, many people can point to alive and active parents, older relatives, and friends. Within dioceses and religious congregations, older priests, sisters, and brothers labor in ministry and are vibrant within the community. A number of young adults think: death will happen to all of them before it catches up with me. About midlife, this attitude changes. If parents are still alive they are also becoming more dependent. The same is true of older relatives, friends, priests, sisters, and brothers. The buffer generation's strength is diminishing. Worse yet, many midlifers realize slowly that a younger generation now looks to them as a new buffer generation.

The newspaper's obituary column also offers midlifers conclusive and disturbing evidence of the reality of death. People appear to be dying at a younger age. More alarming, many midlifers discover the more dead they know, the more living it seems they do not know. As one grows older, contemporaries are more likely to die. Their death, however, is unexpected and comes as a shock. Midlifers realize that if others their age are dying through accident or ill health, it could also happen to them. They become more concerned with health, diet, weight, and exercise.

Finally, many people in the middle years have an "Oh my God" experience. It develops along these lines: out late at a party but needing to rise early the following morning, you respond slowly to the alarm and wander into the bathroom to wash up. Feeling sleepy and tired, you turn on the light. Looking into the mirror you gasp, "Oh my God, is that really me? No, it must be an impostor who moved in where I used to live." The wear and tear of physical decline is difficult for a number of midlife men and women to accept. It was for Bobby Slocum, the fictional middle-aged hero of Joseph Heller's *Something Happened*. Slocum worries about his deterioration. He feels he is moving toward a fulfillment of all the ills of old age. "I am growing forgetful," Slocum tells us, "My eyesight is deteriorating. I wear reading glasses now and require a stronger prescription every year. Periodontal work will save my teeth only for a while. I know I repeat myself at home with my children and my wife . . . soon I will be repeating myself everywhere and be shunned as a prattling old fool."[4] In reality, physicians indicate that at midlife the extent of one's physical and psychological decline is negligible. For many people, though, each greying or shedding hair is a reminder of age and ultimately mortality.

Their awareness of mortality causes people to reorder their perspective of time. They begin to view their life in terms of the time they have left to live. Saul Bellow's fictional character Moses Herzog expresses that experience when he says, "Maybe I am going through a change in outlook." Recalling his mother's death, he realizes that he is "one of the mature generation now, and life was his to do something with, if he could."[5] In crossing the line between early and middle adulthood men and women lose a sense of easy immortality. They know more clearly that they have already lived more years than the number that lie ahead for them. This knowledge makes a critical difference: people are no longer willing to live according to the standards and values of others.

---

4. Joseph Heller, *Something Happened* (New York: Ballantine Books, 1975), p. 402.

5. Saul Bellow, *Herzog* (New York: Viking Press, 1964), pp. 233, 46.

Bridging the gap between early and middle adulthood

The need to bridge the gap between early and middle adulthood is another reason that the transition at midlife is so important.[6] Midlife brings new roles and responsibilities. A middle-aged priest may be faced with his first assignment as pastor of a parish. Now a member of the senior generation, he has decision-making responsibilities and opportunities for creating a vision of the Church. A religious sister in midlife finds that she thinks about administering a school or coordinating her community. She notices that others look to her for leadership and direction. Unlike a young person responsible only to an older generation or an elderly person who nurtures a younger generation, the middle-aged sister, brother, or priest is responsible to both younger and older generations. Many midlife people feel "squeezed" by these two generations. They must offer more emotional nurturance to others than at any other time during life. One religious sister expressed her dilemma this way: "Sometimes I feel like the community car. You serve everyone, but nobody bothers to check your oil, fill your gas tank, or provide regular maintenance. Who's going to take care of me?" This middle position also presents other difficulties. Looking at an older generation, midlife people sometimes see what they do not want to become. Comparing themselves with younger community members, they mourn the loss of vitality and youthful promise.

Some middle-aged religious professionals also find themselves reevaluating their relationships or grieving their lack of them. Many report fewer friends than earlier in life. Others commit themselves to work on relationships that are important to them.

During the midlife transition men and women again reevaluate their early Dream. They discover how they have fulfilled it or neglected it in their life. For those who spent early adulthood becoming somebody rather than doing something they loved, their victory now seems hollow. People begin to ask themselves: What have I done with my life? What have I done with myself?

---

6. See Levinson, *Seasons of a Man's Life,* pp. 191-208.

What are my greatest talents, and how am I using them or wasting them? What do I truly give to and get from other people? Is it possible for me to live in a way that best combines my talents, current desires, values, and aspirations? During this period, people come to terms with their past and prepare for the future. In doing so, they question virtually every aspect of their life. As in every transition, termination and initiation are essential to this process.

In *The Arrangement,* Elia Kazan tells the story of Eddie Anderson, a man who has lost all touch with his Greek heritage to the point of changing his name from Evangelah to Edwin and eventually to Eddie to satisfy the tempo and life-style of the California advertising firm in which he becomes an executive.[7] More important, in the process Eddie also betrays his Dream of becoming a writer. He marries a woman who fits in with the betrayal of his Dream and develops friends and a life pattern that almost choke his Dream to death. In the final analysis, Eddie Anderson's entire life becomes an *arrangement.*

Eddie's tale begins just after he has almost killed himself in an automobile accident. He himself is unsure that it was actually an accident. As Eddie's story unfolds, the reader finds example after example of his betrayal of his Dream. Although sexually intimate with a number of women, he is emotionally intimate with no one. His writing talents have been twisted into churning out advertising copy. One day, Eddie quits—his job, marriage, life-style, and life direction. Predictably, his contemporaries are frightened and view him as being out of his mind. His wife attempts to have him declared insane, and the family lawyer is sent to talk some sense into him. The story of Eddie Anderson is, in the end, the tale of one man's attempt to return to the spirit of his early Dream and rework it into his life so that he is not tyrannized by its adolescent aspects but instead revitalized by its life.

What about the midlife religious professional's Dream? A number of priests, brothers, and sisters arrive at their middle years and find that their life also is an arrangement. Having strayed some distance from their early Dream, they feel empty,

---

7. Elia Kazan, *The Arrangement* (New York: Stein, 1967).

angry, used, and frustrated. They wonder what happened to their early ideals, their hopes for the future, their vision of what their life would become. For example, instead of developing a vibrant spiritual life many have become workaholics. Rather than finding support from their relationships with others and their God, they are burned out. Discouraged and disillusioned, a number of midlife religious professionals conclude their only salvation is escape. These feelings are a normal and necessary part of the transition at midlife. They force people to deal with the challenges of the period.

Like Anderson, and most other people, religious and priests face several developmental tasks at midlife. Their first task is to deal with the disparity between who they are and who they once dreamed of becoming. Those failing to realize their cherished dreams must come to terms with their disappointment and settle on new choices around which to build their lives. Others who realized some of their early hopes and dreams now need to consider the meaning and value of their success. Midlife religious professionals might have to mourn the person they have not and now may never become. Their grief work will help them to integrate better the tragic and romantic aspects of their life. They learn the consequences of their life decisions. With each choice made, other opportunities are lost, some forever. For example, in choosing to be a religious sister, a woman also chooses not to spend her life primarily with one other person. At midlife, married women also reflect on the consequences of their life decision. At times they may wonder what life would be like if they had not chosen to marry a particular man and mother children. Questions such as these are expected during any life transition. In reappraising their lives, midlife men and women must ask: What is the fate of my youthful dreams? What possibilities exist for change in the future?

During midlife, adults also face the task of demythologizing themselves.[8] Young men and women need to believe they are larger than life so they can ambition what is expected and asked of them. At midlife, though, they need to de-illusion themselves.

---

8. See Levinson, *Seasons of a Man's Life,* pp. 192-93.

This process dispels their false sense of enchantment and helps them face their own personal poverty and limitations: limits of energy, talents, dreams, resources, and time. In doing so, people recognize that some of their beliefs about themselves and the workings of their world are simply not true. For example, they are not innocents; their loved ones are not immune from sickness and death; justice does not always earn justice in return. This work of disenchantment gives rise to a myriad of feelings: disappointment, grief, sadness, and depression, but also wonder and a sense of freedom. The experience is similar to losing a family member or friend through death. The mourning takes time. Just as one's relationship with a loved one is not ended by death, the relationship with oneself does not end at midlife; rather, one is transformed through the process of disenchantment.

Men and women who refuse the challenge of de-illusioning themselves often become *dis*illusioned. They cannot accept their limits and instead insist that they, their world, and other people be as they imagine them to be. Failing to let go of past understandings, these people risk having their cherished notions taken away. Stripped of their precious beliefs and values, they are left estranged and end up bitter and cynical.

Some sisters, brothers, and priests choose to become disillusioned rather than de-illusioned. Consider the brother who complains, "This is not the community I once joined." His belief is clear: the world should not change. In refusing to surrender this notion, this man avoids the transition's challenge. Another religious professional fails to let go of a false image of himself. He cannot, for example, accept the limits of his administrative abilities. When others criticize, he becomes an angry victim and withdraws, engages in self-pity, and collects injustices. At midlife, his developmental failures further erode his self-image. Still other religious professionals choose a "geographical cure." Rather than face their limits, these men and women conclude their difficulty has little to do with them. Instead, it is due to their life situation, relationships, ministry, assignment, or co-workers. These people move from assignment to assignment or from community to community in search of an ideal situation.

Some eventually learn the wisdom of a recently divorced man who quipped, "Sometimes I fantasize about hopping on a jet, flying to South America, and starting a whole new life for myself. The trouble is that I know I'll be waiting for me when I get off the plane."

Midlife adults' third major task is to work more seriously than before to become individuals.[9] Carl Jung called this effort the process of individuation and highlighted two important aspects: the limited growth of the individual during early adulthood and the unique opportunities for human development at midlife. He observed that in spite of changes people go through during their twenties and thirties, most arrive at midlife not much different from the person they were in their early twenties. The transition at midlife, however, gives them a chance to make more serious life changes and to chart new directions. This work of individuation is expedited when people pursue the tasks of developing, reconciling, and integrating their various polarities.

Archetypes foster development

A polarity is an archetype, an image established over thousands of generations that comes to exist in every person's mind. Young/old, for example, is a polarity. As a consequence, the terms "young" and "old" characterize a great deal more than their chronological meaning. "Young" is an archetypal symbol that has many meanings: birth, possibility, openness, and energy. "Old" represents stability, fruition, and completion. Archetypes have both attractive and unattractive aspects. To be young, for instance, is to be lively, growing, and heroic. It can also imply impulsivity and a lack of experience. Being old can mean to be wise, influential, and mature but also tyrannical and unconnected to life.

Jung observed that developing one's archetypes is an important part of becoming an individual. They either develop to a

9. See Carl Jung, *Modern Man in Search of a Soul,* trans. W. S. Dell and Cary F. Baynes (New York: Harcourt, Brace and World, 1933), pp. 95-115.

high degree or remain dormant. Archetypes evolve in every person from rather undifferentiated ideas into increasingly complex internal images and give a person the potential for further development. For instance, when people consider their image of God, they find (if they have worked to develop this archetype) that it is much more complex and differentiated in their adult years than it was when they were six or seven years old.

Four of Jung's polarities are important for this discussion: young/old; separate/attached; creative/destructive; and masculine/feminine. The development and integration of the first helps us surrender false self-images, the second influences our spiritual life, the third is useful for resolving lifelong angers, and the last is an invisible partner in many of our relationships.

Young/old

As part of every transition, people create a new integration of the young/old polarity appropriate for their time in life.[10] They work on these internal figures and place them in a new balance. At midlife, this work gives rise to a genuine self-image, allowing people to mentor others and leave a legacy.

The experience of being old stimulates the transition's onset. People complain, for example, about feeling stagnant and in a rut. At this point men and women are faced with one of two choices: begin a period of transition or avoid this challenge. By choosing growth, they are challenged with the complexity of their developmental work. At times, their life will appear wasted and empty. On other occasions, they will discover new and exciting possibilities within themselves and others. As the transition comes to a close, "young" thoughts about being born again appear.

For the midlifer, this death-to-life experience is one of personal conversion. People de-illusion themselves and accept the death of their youthful self-image as hero or heroine. They also discover that there are some heroic qualities they can keep and that some new ones develop that help shape their middle-aged hero or heroine. Many changes accompany their growth. The

---

10. See Levinson, *Seasons of a Man's Life,* pp. 209-21.

"old" qualities of judgment, breadth of perspective, and integration increase. Youth's energy and imagination become a source of vitality.

Those who avoid the challenge of integration cling to youth or become prematurely old and lacking in youthful qualities. A man of forty, for example, may act quite immaturely. He attempts to be young in the manner and style of an eighteen-year-old. Another person takes on heavy adult responsibilities too early in life. In failing to integrate the young/old polarity at midlife, she misses the opportunity to explore, develop, or evaluate her Dream, and her youthful passions remain stifled.

To achieve a balance between young and old is not an easy task. At midlife, however, people have an optimal opportunity to do so. If successful, they also create a legacy for future generations. This developmental accomplishment is an important one. Most people seek reassurance that their life has made a difference. They want to contribute to future generations. Lacking conventional means for leaving a legacy, religious professionals need to address this task in creative ways. The mentoring role offers one a way to contribute to the future of humankind. Both parents and peers, mentors facilitate the Dreams of others. The ministry of priests, sisters, and brothers creates an opportunity for this role by providing situations in which they can encourage other people and support the development of their Dream. In doing so, religious professionals leave an important part of themselves with others, a legacy more lasting than money, buildings, and monuments.

Separate/attached

Developing their separate/attached polarity enables people to deal with issues of solitude and belonging. The term "attachment" encompasses all those forces that tie men and women to their environment. Belonging to their external world, people care about it, hate it, or find it confusing, interesting, or frightening. They demonstrate their attachment when they try to master, adapt to, or participate in their world.

Separateness is the opposite of attachment. It takes place when people are involved primarily in their inner world. This experience is not the same as loneliness or isolation. People suffer loneliness or isolation when, attached to their external world, they are also cut off from it in some way. For example, a man who is physically alone yet actively involved with his resentment over past injustices is still firmly attached to his external world.

During early adulthood, men and women are more concerned with the belonging side of the polarity. It is important for young adults to achieve membership in their society and to be affirmed as part of it. It is a devastating experience for young people when they are not accepted by their peers.

At midlife, however, men and women need to understand their own solitude. Many fear it because society equates solitude with loneliness, but the two states are quite different. More important, in fleeing from solitude people forfeit their chance of discovering many aspects of themselves and their life with God.

In moving toward greater solitude, people also become less dependent on others. They achieve a better balance between their needs and those of society. In attending to themselves in a way that is not self-centered, men and women become less controlled by their ambitions and dependencies. Hence, they contribute to society in a more selfless manner. Simply stated, to be able to care deeply for others, people must also care deeply about themselves. This caring, however, concerns itself with human development and integrity rather than material possessions.

New understandings and images needed in the spiritual life

People who seek solitude also create an opportunity to develop their spiritual life. Separateness fosters one type of spiritual growth by making room for life's spiritual question: On whom or what do I set my heart? It also quiets the prayer of midlife men and women. This greater silence in prayer enhances their sensitivity to God's presence in their life. During early adulthood, prayer is often noisy and externally oriented. At midlife, in becoming more reflective, people use prayer to journey homeward toward themselves and the God in their inner depths.

Many men and women are surprised that attention to the polarity's separate side also affects belonging. Having struggled to achieve quiet and an inward focus in their personal prayer, they can now engage more fully in social prayer. Eucharist and community prayer are enriched. A balance has been achieved between private and social prayer.

At the same time that faith is shaped by the initiatives of grace and the Spirit, the integration of the separate/attached polarity provides fertile ground for the Holy Spirit's movement in people's lives. At every major life transition men and women are presented with the opportunity to shape the new era's life structure and to find new, enriching ways of being in faith. They will fail if they insist on clinging rigidly to their prior understandings of faith and images of God. In developing and integrating the separate/attached polarity, men and women must take the opportunity to complete this task successfully.[11]

Creative/destructive polarity and lifelong angers

The creative/destructive polarity and its resolution have serious implications for a person's lifelong angers. Each individual has the power not only to be tremendously creative but to hurt and destroy others intentionally or unintentionally. In the course of life, men and women will hurt others and will in turn be hurt by them. During the transition at midlife they must come to terms with this reality and with their grievances against others for perceived injustices. Again, this process involves mourning and a letting go. Failure to undertake this process gives rise to persons who refuse to surrender lifelong hurts and who continue a romance with perceived injustices long after midlife and into their mature years. Their energy and creativity are sapped by their rage and self-righteous indignation. As "angry martyrs," they ultimately turn their destructiveness on themselves.

---

11. For additional discussion of spirituality and the life cycle, see Gerald O'Collins, *The Second Journey* (Ramsey, N.J.: Paulist Press, 1978), and James Fowler, *Stages of Faith* (San Francisco: Harper and Row, 1981).

To exercise effective leadership, men and women must also integrate their creative/destructive polarity. Provincial superiors act destructively when they make decisions that disappoint members of their congregations. A particular sister, for example, feels that she is well suited to be the administrator of a school. After all, she has the necessary degrees and is certified in school administration. The provincial, however, realizes that if she appoints this woman she will also have to search out a new faculty. Credentials aside, this potential principal does not relate well with other people. The provincial appoints another woman to the administrative postition. In doing so, she is acting destructively. However unintentionally, she has hurt someone. Effective leadership, at times, demands decisions that will disappoint and hurt some people. Those in leadership unwilling to make these difficult decisions should resign. If they attempt to please everyone, leaders ultimately satisfy few people and also hurt the group. Those who avoid difficult decisions fail to integrate the creative/destructive polarity. In denying their destructive side, they paralyze their leadership ability and capacity to approach their work creatively.

What about the sister who was refused the administrative position? It would be helpful if she could express her disappointment and anger. This admission may bring to the surface any possible underlying fears of rejection and incompetency. Mistaken notions about anger, though, cause many religious and priests to repress or deny this feeling. Instead of dealing with it, they push their anger underground. Consider those who relate the details of an injustice done to them with such feeling and rage that an observer is sure the situation took place recently. Only later does it become clear that the circumstances discussed happened fifteen years ago and most of the players are dead.

Other people deal with their disappointment, anger, and destructiveness passively. They obstruct and undermine the efforts of others. These men and women eventually become mired in their rage. Denying their own destructive side, they also undermine their creative potential.

Masculine/feminine

"It all goes back, of course, to Adam and Eve," says psychologist Carol Gilligan, "a story which shows, among other things, that if you make a woman out of a man, you are bound to get into trouble."[12] Men and women are different in a number of ways. Women, for example, tend to operate out of an ethic of care. They focus on the necessary interdependence of people. In contrast, many men center on self-fulfillment. Some see care from others as interference.

The differences between men and women are more complicated than they appear at first. Every person is evidently androgynous, both masculine and feminine. A man has an unconscious feminine side; a woman, an unconscious masculine side. Although each side of the polarity has both positive and negative aspects, each enlivens the individual.

To establish relationships of intimacy, people need to develop and integrate their masculine/feminine polarity.[13] Because of this fact and the considerable attention this polarity has received in recent years, it will be discussed more completely than the other three polarities.

If people are both masculine and feminine, why has this fact eluded them for so many years? To begin with, many people give little importance to self-knowledge. Only when in much pain and confusion do they struggle for self-understanding. Even when in great pain, some men and women choose to live meaningless lives rather than embrace the process of coming to know themselves. Next, some aspects of people generally defy self-knowledge. These shadow aspects, often obvious to other people, are unknown to their owners. Finally, men and women lack

---

12. See "Sexes: Attuned to Different Voices," in the *Washington Post,* January 11, 1983 (Carol Krucoff's interview with Carol Gilligan).

13. An excellent discussion of the masculine/feminine polarity is included in John Sanford's *The Invisible Partners* (New York: Paulist Press, 1980).

knowledge of their feminine and masculine sides respectively because these aspects are typically projected onto others. Consequently, they see these qualities as belonging to other people and having little to do with them.

The development and integration of the masculine/feminine polarity are important for at least two reasons: to understand and discard sexual stereotypes; and to establish relationships of intimacy. With regard to the first reason, the terms masculine and feminine refer to the *meaning* of gender and not to biological gender. Every culture has its gender images. In America little boys are taught not to cry, while their female counterparts are warned against being tomboys. The indoctrination with gender images begins very early.

Rigid adherence to these images can give rise to skewed psychological and emotional development. Totally masculine men may be unable to be emotionally close to women because they regard them as either maternal or sexual, but not both. These men are also often unable to be intimate with other men. The "Marlboro man" is a case in point: for some, he is a characterization of the American male hero, a loner in need of no one. Today the Marlboro man seldom rides the plains in cigarette commercials; in magazines and on billboards all over the country he more often looks as though he shops for clothes at Bloomingdale's and has his hair styled by Vidal Sassoon. Nonetheless, the loner image of detachment and a hard, tough exterior remains.

The stereotypical woman is presented as seductive or dimwitted. Either she is used as a ploy to increase sales of the Mercury Bobcat car or her ideas are grouped with the babblings of television's Edith Bunker. These characterizations highlight a failure to develop and reconcile the masculine/feminine polarity. Although the women's movement and the more nascent men's movement may eventually help eradicate these stereotypes, it would be foolhardy to believe that the barriers have been torn down when consciousness has merely been raised a little.

Integration required for intimacy

The second reason for developing and integrating the masculine/feminine polarity—to establish intimate relationships—is quite important.[14] The transition at midlife appears to provide optimal conditions for undertaking this task successfully. In early adulthood, for instance, men often experience their feminine side as dangerous, while women do not want to be thought of as too masculine. Young women may shrink from expressing their natural assertiveness and competence because their masculine side is too threatening to them, while young men fear the implications of their more intuitive qualities.

During their twenties and thirties, a number of men see a danger in intimacy. At the same time, many women are threatened by separation. When a man gets close to a woman his sense of masculinity is sometimes threatened. Scared by intimacy, he moves away. A woman, threatened by separation, moves closer. In young adulthood, then, some men have difficulty with relationships while a number of women experience problems trying to become an individual.

When people have seriously confronted their own eventual mortality, they seem less concerned with the demands of gender images. Before this happens, young men may keep an emotional distance from women because they are reminded of their own feminine side. Along the same lines, many women try to define themselves solely through their relationships and connections to other people. To stand alone is to come face to face with their own masculine side.

Because one's unconscious masculine or feminine side presents such a threat, its traits are often projected onto others. When people project some aspect of the self, it is perceived as being outside themselves, as though it pertained to someone else and had little or nothing to do with them. The reality of the other person becomes obscured by the projection, and he or she becomes either overvalued or undervalued. For example, when

---

14. The remarks in this section are confined to relationships between men and women. For a limited treatment of projection and homosexuality, see Sanford's *The Invisible Partners,* pp. 94-99.

the positive aspects of a man's feminine side are projected onto a woman, she becomes highly desirable to him. She is the object of his erotic fantasies and sexual longings, and he believes that he would be fulfilled if only he could be with her and make love to her. Although flattering at first to some women, this situation may eventually become suffocating. As the woman attempts to develop her own personality in the relationship, she may find that the man begins to project negative parts of his unconscious feminine side onto her and to blame her for his moods and unhappiness. The fact is that the man has been relating to his projection and not to a real person.

By contrast, when a woman projects her unconscious masculine side onto a man, she sees him as a guide, savior, and hero. She feels as though she can be complete only through him. Yet once the relationship is viewed realistically, the savior becomes the infuriating and frustrating man responsible for all the woman's disappointments and feelings of belittlement.

Projection produces infatuations

Both these situations involving projection have very little to do with actual love or intimacy. Instead, they are states of mutual fascination and infatuation. As such, they are valuable preludes to the expansion of one's personality and emotional life. However, relationships founded exclusively on infatuation cannot last. To the extent that people's relationships are founded on projection, they are in love with aspects of themselves.

Real love is between real people, not projections. To assist one another in the discovery and development of their unconscious masculine/feminine polarity, people have to become vulnerable to one another. Only in this way is intimacy possible. The word intimacy here has a specific meaning: allowing another person to come close enough to me so that I could possibly change. More and more in American society, people encounter each other sexually before coming to know each other in a broader and deeper sense. Although some people may be comfortable with such sexual and physical intimacy, they are neophytes at the harder but more rewarding work of psychological, emotional, and spiritual intimacy. Falling in love, or infatuation, is only a step toward intimacy. When the infatuation dissolves and the other person emerges as he or she really is, then intimacy is possible.

In intimate relationships people accept responsibility for their own happiness and unhappiness; they neither expect another person to make them happy nor blame the other for their bad moods, frustrations, or problems. The state of intimacy is optimal for discovering one's masculine or feminine side. At midlife, for example, a number of men discover through a relationship the importance of intimacy, relationships, and care about others. This knowledge is something that many women came to earlier in life. Middle-aged women, likewise, stop trying in their relationships to be selfless in a self-destructive way. Many women judge themselves within the context of their ability to care for others. At midlife, however, they come to question their old notion that the way to sustain relationships is to take care of other people. As a result, many start to articulate directly what they want and need. These women realize that one of the people it is important not to hurt is themselves.

Failure to integrate the masculine/feminine polarity has several consequences. A man who is out of touch with his unconscious feminine side appears sulky, overly sensitive, and withdrawn. Acting peevish and depressed, he is unavailable for relationships. This man's speech is peppered with sarcasm, innuendo, and poisonous jabs that sometimes pass for humor. Such behavior may result from a number of factors. First of all, his work may drain him and leave little room for his emotional life. Also, he might have difficulty expressing his feelings. As a consequence, they fall into his unconscious and are expressed indirectly in moodiness and covertly hostile actions.

If a man's unconscious feminine side is the master of his moods, then a woman's unconscious masculine side is the master of her opinions. It reflects itself in the "shoulds" and "oughts" of a woman's "critics' committee." The negative aspects of a woman's unconscious masculine side include judgments, critical statements, and generalizations that do not spring from her own process of thinking and feeling. Instead, they have been picked up from various authoritative sources: parents, Church, superiors, and books and articles. If these negative aspects get projected onto others, the result is a woman who is blunt and always critical of others. Those women who project the opinions of their unconscious masculine side onto themselves are robbed of their creativity and feel as though they have nothing to offer anyone.

People need to increase the possibility of intimacy with others. As women and men come to accept their own poles of masculine and feminine, they are capable of genuine intimacy, for the threat of closeness and independence is lessened. Every relationship needs a balance between individuality and togetherness. Thus, by integrating this polarity and thereby growing in realistic self-knowledge and acceptance, men and women prepare themselves for the developmental tasks of the mature years.

Chapter Six

Final payments

A journalist once asked ninety-year-old George Bernard Shaw how he felt about having reached that age. "Considering the alternative," Shaw answered without hesitation, "it feels very good!" The gallant comments of another old person lack Shaw's sharp wit but contain their own understated humor. "Every morning I wake up in pain," she said, "I wiggle my toes. Good. They still obey. I open my eyes. Good. I can see. Everything hurts, but I get dressed. I walk down to the ocean. Good. It is still there. Now my day can start. About tomorrow, I'll never know. After all, I'm 89. I can't live forever."[1]

The years between the transition at midlife and a person's death can span less than one or more than several decades. Jung described this period as the afternoon of life and judged its developmental questions to be chiefly spiritual. Although a number of men and women enter life's second half naively feeling well prepared, they learn quickly that skills and beliefs suitable for the morning of life are found wanting after age forty. Jung described well the midlifer's dilemma:

> Thoroughly unprepared we take the step into the afternoon of life; worse still, we take this step with the false presumption that our truths and ideals will serve us as hitherto. But we cannot live the afternoon of life according to the programme of

---

1. These comments appear in Barbara Myerhoff's anthropological study of aging in a southern California community. See Barbara Myerhoff, *Number Our Days* (New York: E. P. Dutton, 1978).

life's morning—for what was great in the morning will be little
at evening, and what in the morning was true will at evening
become a lie.[2]

The afternoon of life includes three eras: middle, late, and
late, late adulthood. As Americans live longer, more and more
of them are moving through the creative and productive years of
middle adulthood into the last two eras of the life cycle. Each era
has its own developmental tasks. Midlife religious, for example,
need to expand their care for others, increase their interiority,
and achieve greater effectiveness in ministry.[3] Retirement,
changing roles, and decreased energy and stamina challenge men
and women during late adulthood. Those in late, late adulthood
face still other tasks: adjusting to less independence, chronic
physical and psychological decline, and the death of lifelong
friends.

Less preoccupied with the youth-oriented culture of the recent
past, today's religious professionals are shifting their attention
to life's afternoon. The news about this period is indeed good.
More and more people testify that in many ways life does begin
at forty. As men and women develop a more realistic self-image,
a new self-understanding evolves. They deal more effectively
with the physical and psychological difficulties that come with
aging. Life's afternoon, now a subject for serious study, has
become less frightening.

In this chapter, I will examine life after the transition at midlife. To do so, I will describe the developmental tasks faced by
men and women in middle, late, and late, late adulthood, and
discuss the problems that surround retirement from ministry.
Finally, I will examine the difficulties brought about by the
physical and psychological decline that is oftentimes part of the
process of aging.

---

2. Jung, *Modern Man in Search of a Soul,* p. 108.
3. See Whitehead and Whitehead, *Christian Life Patterns,* pp. 114-32.

Middle adulthood

At about age forty-five the midlife transition is concluded.[4]
Entering middle adulthood, men and women face three challenging developmental tasks. They need to develop greater care
for others, interiority, and effectiveness in ministry. This first
task, expanding their capacity to care for others, is crucial
because they are caught between two generations, responsible
for both younger and older men and women. An adequate supply of self-esteem and an established identity assist people in
meeting the stress of their new responsibilities. One major
reason for this stress is that middle-aged people often have little
opportunity to choose those for whom they will be responsible
or how this task will be carried out.

As the number of older sisters, priests, and brothers increases,
middle-aged religious professionals search for creative ways to
care for their needs. They also feel stretched by the many demands and responsibilities placed upon them. Religious leaders
especially feel the strain. Some pastors, for example, find themselves taxed by the presence and personality of a pastor emeritus
who is experiencing difficulty adjusting to the limits of his new
role. Provincial superiors feel overwhelmed by the growing demands of their community's apostolates in the face of the
group's limited finances, dwindling resources, and members'
personal needs. These leaders identify easily with David Campbell's cogent question, "If I'm in charge here why is everybody
laughing?"[5]

Mentoring relationships offer midlifers a unique opportunity
to expand their capacity to care for others. Effective mentors
care for other people without manipulating them. Exercising this

4. See Daniel J. Levinson, "Toward a Conception of the Adult Life
Course," in Neil J. Smelser and Erik H. Erikson, eds., *Themes of
Work and Love in Adulthood* (Cambridge: Harvard University Press,
1980), pp. 265-90.

5. For a brief and delightful treatment of some of the difficulties of
contemporary leadership, see David Campbell's *If I'm in Charge Here
Why is Everybody Laughing?* (Allen, Texas: Argus Communications,
1980).

role with both younger and older generations, middle-aged mentors have as their primary responsibility the facilitation of the Dreams of other men and women. With a younger generation, the application of this principle is straightforward. Mentors aid young people by providing them with encouragement and, at times, a life worthy of emulation. In benefiting from the relationship, those mentored develop their Dream and shed some of its adolescent tyranny. The adolescent Dream is by necessity idealistic and accentuates only one aspect of a person. Over time, people let go of their Dream's tyrannical aspects. In doing so, they also rediscover neglected parts of themselves. Mentoring relationships help them to accomplish these tasks.

The task of mentoring an older generation is not so clearly defined. However, some general guidelines do exist. First of all, mentors can help older people rediscover parts of themselves lost when they made past decisions. In deciding on previous life choices, men and women by necessity neglected aspects of their personality. During life's second half they can rediscover their forgotten gifts. Truman Capote's evocative phrase, "other voices, other rooms" frames the experience of many older people as they listen to and search out parts of themselves that need to be integrated into their life fabric. A bishop, for example, is faced with a sixty-year-old priest in failing health. Until recently, this man was a successful pastor. Although not completely incapacitated, he needs to reduce his parish involvement dramatically. The appointment of an administrator for the parish would relieve this man's daily work load but do little to help him adjust to his new circumstances. As a mentor, the bishop can help this priest explore his unrealized talents, early Dream, and those contributions made already. The bishop can also help him to be realistic about his present strengths and abilities. In working together over time, both men can benefit from the relationship: the bishop by mentoring, the pastor by assuming a position wherein he can rediscover his talents and use them for the Church while still caring for his limited health.

Another religious superior mentors a retired sister in search of a "second career." Fearful that she will be unsuccessful in her search, this woman questions her decision to resign from teaching. She is frightened by the prospect of job interviews, wonders what additional education she might need, and, at times, regresses and insists she is incapable of gathering any additional information about those ministries suitable for her. The provincial can assist this woman by encouraging her during this difficult time. To infantilize her by doing all the necessary work of search and exploration, however, is a betrayal of the mentoring role. To do so reinforces the fear of failure already so alive in this woman. Middle-aged mentors need to be guides and supports, not rescuers and saviors.

Around age forty a second aspect of middle adulthood's developmental work gets under way. At this time people experience an increased need to develop their interior life. This desire is especially true for priests, sisters, and brothers. They leave the often compulsive, unreflective business of their apostolate and once more become explorers of the world within. Some of them need time off from ministry, a break in routine, an opportunity for conversion. Even though religious and priestly life should provide men and women with the structure and time to develop their interior life over all the years of adulthood, many religious professionals come to middle adulthood and find an emptiness within. Their journey homeward to themselves begins only in midlife and continues throughout the remainder of the life cycle. For some people, a spiritual awakening sets this journey in motion. Others discover that the reality of their eventual death, questions about their life's meaning, or a profound experience of change redirects them toward their interior life. A middle-aged religious sister, for example, about to celebrate the twenty-fifth anniversary of her vows wonders whom she will invite. An author and lecturer, she is quite successful in her work and well respected by her colleagues. However, she has no personal friends, no relationships of intimacy, only colleagues and acquaintances. In discovering this fact, she also reevaluates her life commitment, work, life-style, and priorities. The process is a painful one. She feels fragmented and finds that in addition to her lack of personal friends, she has also neglected her interior life. As she turns her sights away from the external world and toward her inner world, this woman does not need to discover something new in her life but rather to see her life in a new way. She needs to reorder her priorities, develop genuine relationships, attend to her interior life, make changes in her life-style, and begin to take care of herself.

Finally, during middle adulthood religious professionals can become more effective in their ministry. At different times in the life cycle, religious and priests are called to various expressions of ministry. Early in adult life, for example, they have high ideals and an abundance of energy. If, in their enthusiasm, young sisters, brothers, and priests claim to work fifteen to sixteen hours a day, believe them. They are probably modest in their report. This early period of ministry is one of discipleship, during which people serve their Church most often as followers. Their dioceses and religious communities provide them with opportunities to develop their skills and test out their resources and dreams of generous service. The many opportunities available for energetic and short-term service to God's people draw on the idealism of these young ministers and the provisional and exploratory nature of this period in the life cycle. At midlife, however, these men and women take their skills and resources and use them in a new way for God's people. They need to move from the role of follower to that of leader in the community. Such a change increases the effectiveness of their ministry.[6]

Transition around age fifty

Another period of transition begins around age fifty. Similar to the one occurring at about age thirty, this time for second thoughts lasts four to five years on the average. For many people, it is a relatively smooth and undramatic period. Continuing along the same general life path, they use the period to make minor changes in their life structure. For some, the seriousness and responsibilities of middle adulthood have become apparent, and they assess their success in dealing creatively with the period's developmental tasks. For others, the reality of their own death, though not imminent, is clearer. Many people

---

6. See Whitehead and Whitehead, *Christian Life Patterns*, pp. 138-40.

wonder what they must change or adjust in order to bring their life more into line with the spirit of their early Dream. Mentoring relationships are evaluated, the opportunities for leaving a legacy considered, and progress on developing an interior life measured. It is generally a time for readjustments, not for revolution.

Successful transitional work around age fifty is crucial for a number of reasons. Most important, it permits people to achieve even greater actualization of their capabilities and virtues, and allows them to make further contributions to their society. Stated simply, the developmental work of the period assists people to grow in wisdom and thus fulfill the Talmud's observation that whereas forty is the age of "understanding," fifty is the time for "giving counsel."

What about those men and women who failed to examine themselves or make necessary changes during the transitions at midlife or earlier? For them, the age-fifty transition can be one of moderate to severe crisis. Having failed to examine themselves and make necessary adjustments throughout life, these people now feel trapped. They also have a growing awareness of their limited life span. As a result, they have many regrets about their life but feel also that it is too late to change. Disillusionment often results.

People who avoided their developmental work during previous transitions are often frightened when they face it for the first time at the end of their fifth decade. Some of them will first blame others for their predicament. Embittered and self-centered, they argue that if they had only known years ago what it is they know now, they would have made any necessary adjustments and changes in themselves and their lives. They insist that it is too late to do so now. In reality, it is never too late to make adjustments in the life structure. Consider the religious brother who arrives at age fifty having allowed himself little psychological, emotional, and spiritual development during previous transitional times. Unable to mourn past losses, or to accept development as part of life, he is embittered by the many changes that have taken place in the brotherhood. No longer does this style of life provide status or security. Leadership betrays him by encouraging new ministerial involvements rather than the congregation's traditional apostolic works. Even community life has changed, and his years with the congregation appear to count for little with younger members. In thinking about his life he feels cheated and angry. With his present knowledge he concludes that he would make other choices if he had his life to live over again. Now, however, age and fears about competency are forcing him to live out his remaining years within the community. Is there any way to help this man grow as he moves through his age-fifty transition?

First of all, assisting this man will not be easy. Professional counseling and later spiritual direction may, at times, be required. Although he needs support and compassion, his disagreeable nature more often causes others to avoid him. His own behavior is the source of his isolation and loneliness.

Furthermore, any rewards gained by helping this brother to grow and develop a real identity will be a long time in coming. His present difficulties were several decades in the making, therefore considerable time will be required for the process of growth to take place.

Finally, it is helpful to remember that men like him are often disagreeable because they are frightened. They fear they cannot change, that there is not enough time to do so, and that they lack the resources to accomplish the work of the transition and make a new beginning. Although the challenge of aiding this man is a great one, it is worth the effort. A wealth of patience, understanding, time, and perseverance are the ingredients necessary for even modest success.

The transition around age fifty, then, is another opportunity for growth. Men and women move away from this period into a time of relative stability. They build a life structure in which to complete the tasks of middle adulthood and prepare for their transition into late adulthood.

Late adulthood

As people move through their late fifties and into their early sixties, they often notice a slight decline in their physical and psychological abilities. One religious sister remarked, for example, that at age sixty she felt "old" for the first time in her life. All of a sudden, life seemed to be over. Other people moving toward late adulthood notice that their memory for names and faces is less dependable, their eyesight and hearing less acute, and their stamina less robust. People have mixed feelings about these changes. Some men and women accept them as part of the process of aging. They turn some of their attention to maintaining their health and to compensating for physical and psychological decline. Others take offense at any suggestion that they are "slowing down." Even though they have moderated their activities and involvements, most people about age sixty feel they still have a great deal to offer others and anticipate a number of productive years ahead of them.

People approach the transition into late adulthood in a variety of ways. Personality and long-standing styles of life determine, in part, their way of dealing with the aging process and events such as retirement.[7] For example, throughout early and middle adulthood a religious sister involved herself in ministry to the detriment of her personal and spiritual life and the formation of friendships. Moving toward retirement, this woman feels cheated. Without friends, avocations, personal interests, and a spiritual life, her future appears grim. Another sister developed many aspects of her personality and struggled throughout life to achieve a balance between ministry, spirituality, relationships, and personal pursuits. As this woman approaches sixty-five, she looks forward to the additional time that a reduced ministry schedule will provide.

The transition into late adulthood has three distinct parts: leaving middle adulthood, crossing the line, and entering late adulthood.[8] To begin with, people leaving middle adulthood undergo a period of life evaluation. Knowing that they have

---

7. See Elaine Brody, "Aging and Family Personality: A Developmental View," *Family Process* 13, no. 1 (March 1974): 29.

8. For a detailed analysis of the late adult years and more specifically issues surrounding retirement, see Golan, *Passing through Transitions,* pp. 190-211.

already lived more years than the number that lie ahead for them, men and women question if they have achieved their life goals. They also evaluate their life performance and resolve conflicts about their failures and disappointments. Finally, they prepare themselves for eventual physical and psychological decline.

At some point late in middle adulthood, people look at their life goals and question whether or not they have completed them. Some priests, sisters, and brothers conclude they have achieved some of the goals they set earlier for themselves. One man, for example, makes his contribution to ministry as a sensitive and capable pastor, another as an effective educator. Both work at a life-style that balances spiritual, emotional, and interpersonal growth. A woman religious attends to her goal of working for justice among the economically and politically oppressed by her choice of ministry and life-style. In general, as people conclude middle adulthood they need to be living a life of integrity. Whatever its shape or specifics, it needs to be a genuine expression of an individual's central nature, beliefs, values, and dreams. As such, in most instances it contributes to society and assures the minister's personal, spiritual, and interpersonal growth.

The death of parents and friends, an outstanding achievement or failure in ministry, and other significant changes often cause people to evaluate their successes and failures in life. When carrying out this task, men and women also attempt to make amends for their mistakes and inadequacies. In accomplishing this work, Church ministers come to accept their life and those who are and have been a part of it as something that had to be and that, by necessity, permitted no substitutions. Stated simply, they take responsibility for their life, insert meaning into it, and actively accept the inevitability of their own life course.

Finally, people prepare for the inevitable decline that accompanies old age by simplifying their life-style, and reflecting more immediately on what it means to die. A sister about age sixty-five, for example, knows that she is closer to death than she was at forty. Although she may live for several more years, her questions about life's meaning are more urgent. There are still tasks to accomplish, life to be lived. Thoughts about death, then, inevitably lead to questions about what it means to have lived. In coming to satisfactory answers, men and women work to integrate the integrity/despair polarity.

Despair expresses the feeling that one's time in life is too short. Not enough is left to start another life or to try out alternate roads to integrity. In contrast, integrity is judging that my life, with all its similarities to the lives of others as well as its idiosyncratic joys and disappointments, could not have been otherwise. Integrity does not eliminate despair; rather, it lives in the face of it. It does not deny that people have regrets and experience guilt about what they have or have not done with their lives. Neither does it insist that all of life's possibilities have been lived out. Integrity also supports the development of wisdom, an essential strength of character. Some wise people are understanding, empathetic, and appreciative of diversity and pluralism. The implicit wisdom of others is displayed more in their actions and attitudes than their words. Still others manifest it in ripened wit and mature judgment. For all these men and women, their wisdom transcends, to some degree, the inevitable diminishments of old age.[9] It also helps older people to continue to contribute to their society.

It is always the old who show younger generations the adequacy of their culture. The real fear of death is not the loss of one's life but rather the loss of meaning. If a particular life commitment and style can support people throughout the life cycle and into old age, then the value and significance of that commitment and life-style are confirmed for all. Erik Erikson captured this notion well when he observed that healthy children will not fear life if their elders have integrity enough not to fear death.

Erikson's observation has important implications for the priesthood and religious life today. If Church ministers arrive at

9. For additional discussion of integrity and despair in old age, see Whitehead and Whitehead, *Christian Life Patterns,* pp. 161-68.

the final years of their life disillusioned and embittered then religious and priestly life will truly have lost significance. Its ability to foster healthy spiritual, personal, and interpersonal development will also be in question. In our present age of transition, older Church ministers are challenged to contribute to the next generation in a way they did not expect. Instead of building upon those models of aging provided for them in years past, they need to create a new one. They must first of all face their personal mortality and in old age surrender their roles and status, possessions, health, and illusions about self and their world. More important, however, they need to grieve and accept the death of old forms of priestly and religious life. Having lived out their days within a structure that is, in many ways, in ruin, they might be tempted to despair. They make a real contribution to the future if, instead, they let go of past forms, embrace the process of mourning, and allow themselves to be converted through it.

The transitional nature of today's Church gives its ministers little choice over what will be lost. As the number of religious professionals becomes smaller and older, security and status are diminished. The closing of parishes, schools, and health care facilities reduces the number of legacies. With changes in dress, style of life, and ministry, former customs and understandings are taken away. In grieving these losses, accepting the confusion and breakdown of the transition's first phase, and moving into the subsequent darkness and exploration, even as they struggle to find the meaning and purpose of their own life, religious professionals moving into late adulthood grow in wisdom and provide those who follow them with a model. Future generations of Church ministers will not be afraid to face the religious and priestly life of the future because these older men and women had integrity enough to accept the loss and death of the present transitional age.

Crossing the line

Retirement from ministry is the single most important event that moves Church ministers over the line from middle into late adulthood. It is also the most crucial change to which many older sisters, priests, and brothers must adapt. As part of this process, old and familiar roles need to be surrendered or adapted in a flexible way, and new ones adopted. A pastor, for example, reduces his parish involvement and moves to the position of pastor emeritus. A once active woman religious elementary school teacher tries now to use the time in her day for tutoring and home visits to senior citizens in her parish.

For retirement to take place smoothly, preparation should begin many years before this event gets under way. To accomplish their work adequately, people need to address three developmental tasks. First, they should recognize retirement as a future possibility and begin to shape their future with it in mind. Next, they need to begin to take active steps to prepare for the event. Finally, people need to make a formal decision about when they will retire and how they will do it.

A number of Church ministers are reluctant to anticipate or prepare for retirement. Some dread the thought, and the large majority tend not to retire easily or at the expected time. A seventy-year-old pastor, for example, protests that he may not live long enough to retire. Another man hopes to avoid cutting back on his involvements and remain totally active all his life.

Preparing for retirement entails far more than planning one's future. People also have to deal with their past and slowly detach themselves from their work roles and those familiar people and places that tie them to a particular ministry. Retirement is a transitional process. There is an ending, an up-in-the-air, and a new beginning phase. Consider the religious sister who concludes her teaching career. She feels the loss of her students, teaching colleagues, even the cafeteria servers and maintenance staff. No longer will her year "start" in September, and she fears that her uncertain future may not be so rewarding as the past. This woman must be willing to grieve her losses and spend time in the fallow emptiness of her transition's middle phase. Only then can she move to the more rewarding circumstances of a new beginning. She might use her talents eventually in a more limited way by tutoring, working in a school office, or assisting with support services such as the audiovisual or library departments. Getting ready for retirement, then, includes the process of anticipatory grieving. It is difficult to leave active ministry and all the affectional and social ties that go with it. We need to begin this process well in advance by reading up on retirement, talking with others about it, and developing our personal interests, spiritual life, relationships, and leisure pursuits.

Adjusting to the time after retirement

Retirement should not be equated with the cessation of ministry. This narrow interpretation fails to take into account the many activities in which retired people engage. Some remain involved in limited ministry roles while others quickly take up substitute activities such as volunteering. This work is carried out in conjunction with leisure pursuits undertaken for self-development and recreational activities that relieve tension.

There are many myths about health and the incidence of death after retirement. In reality, retired people appear to be as healthy or even healthier after they stop working than they were before. Furthermore, retirement does not appear to have a direct effect on mortality or on the frequency of social and psychological problems among older Church ministers.

Some priests, sisters, and brothers adjust well to retirement; others do not. The well-adjusted types include the mature, rocking-chair, and armored retirees.[10] The first group move easily into old age. Relatively free of neurotic conflict they accept themselves realistically and get genuine satisfaction from their activities and personal relationships. Rocking-chair retirees are generally passive and welcome the opportunity to be free of responsibility. For them, this advantage compensates for any disadvantages that old age might bring. Finally, those men and women unable to face passivity or helplessness in late adulthood may be called the armored type of retiree. Their need to keep active is an attempt to ward off their dread of physical decline.

---

10. Well and poorly adjusted types of retirees are described in more detail in Golan, *Passing through Transitions,* pp. 204-205.

Church ministers who are angry or hate themselves generally adjust poorly to retirement. Those who are angry may be bitter over having failed to achieve their earlier life goals. They are unable to reconcile themselves to aging and blame others for their disappointments. The self-haters, feeling depressed, inadequate, and worthless as they grow old, look back on their life with a sense of failure and disappointment, and blame themselves for their misfortunes.

Those men and women in Church ministry who adjust well to retirement manage to stay active within the limits of their health and life circumstances. They visit friends, read, involve themselves in limited ministry, watch television, and develop their hobbies. These men and women feel purposeful and productive and for them late adulthood is a time of stability.

Late, late adulthood

As people move into late, late adulthood physical and mental decline is often more rapid, chronic and catastrophic illness more common, and the death of lifelong friends more frequent. With the onset of their eighties, most Church ministers cease productive work and lose most of their remaining social roles and status. They also face three tasks as they enter the transition into late, late adulthood: they must cope with impaired health; they need to make adjustments in their living situation so as to provide for necessary care; and they must deal with the increasing frequency of death among friends and relatives.

The prevalence of chronic disease increases with age.[11] For example, approximately 85 percent of those people sixty-five years of age or older and living outside of institutions suffer from at least one chronic illness. About 50 percent report some limitation of their normal activities because of a chronic health condition. Although heart disease is the most frequently experienced disability, arthritis, diabetes, varicose veins, asthma, hernias, obesity, hemorrhoids, cataracts, hypertension, and prostate

---

11. For an informative discussion of chronic physical and psychological difficulties that afflict the elderly, see Golan, *Passing through Transitions,* pp. 213-18.

disease are common. A number of the elderly also experience debilitating accidents after some sudden change in their life gives rise to a crisis. Hip fractures among older people, for example, are often related to real or imagined losses such as retirement, the death of a close friend, illness, or a changed living situation.

Physical and mental health appear to be closely related among the elderly. Many neurotic disorders can present themselves as physical disabilities. Consider the elderly woman religious who is depressed. Her condition may present itself as a loss of energy, poor appetite, weight loss, and constipation. Another woman's depression may manifest itself as severe back or neck pain that upon medical examination appears to lack an organic etiology. Depression is probably the principal psychological difficulty experienced by older Church ministers. For many, it causes them to decrease their involvements and gives rise to a gloomy evaluation of their present state and future possibilities, a lack of interest in their surroundings, and strong self-accusations and feelings of guilt over past transgressions.

Paranoid reactions are another common psychological disturbance seen in late, late adulthood. People afflicted with this disorder are suspicious of persons and events around them. At times, they also put together faulty and unrealistic explanations of what happens to them. This distortion of reality is most often due to their effort to "fill in the gaps" in their memory and to deny some of the losses that come with aging. An elderly brother, for example, has difficulty facing the fact that his correspondence has fallen off greatly. He writes less and receives little mail because he is retired and many of those who wrote to him earlier in life are now dead. Unable to accept these facts, he instead accuses others of stealing his mail.

Hypochrondriasis, an excessive preoccupation with bodily functioning, is another disability common among older people. They feel a need to be taken care of and find that having physical complaints is one way to meet this need. Men and women suffering from hypochrondriasis usually have a long list of physical symptoms and complaints. They prefer to dwell on their physical condition and often resent attempts to discuss the psychological factors associated with their complaints.

Finally, sleep disturbances such as less deep sleep, frequent awakenings, and the need for several naps during the daytime, as well as adjustment reactions to change and loss are fairly common among the elderly.

A number of people sixty-five years of age and older with significant mental deficits have an organic brain syndrome, which results from brain-cell damage or malfunction. Men and women so afflicted may be unable to remember what day it is or even where they are living. Others cannot learn new information, fail to remember recent events, lose some ability to think abstractly, and cannot carry out simple sequential tasks such as dressing or setting the table. As the syndrome progresses, self-care can deteriorate, people may begin to lose their way, well-learned material from earlier in life disappears, and the names of family members, fellow religious and priests, and others cannot be recalled. In extreme cases, people may no longer remember their own name and appear confused, perplexed, and bewildered.

Some 10 to 20 percent of the elderly with an organic brain syndrome have a reversible form. A metabolic disturbance or drug intoxication resulting from a faulty medication prescription explains their change in behavior. An elderly priest, for example, may appear confused, drowsy, or incoherent because he is overmedicated. An adjustment in his prescription will return this man to his previous level of functioning. In contrast, the large majority of men and women with an organic brain syndrome have an irreversible form, caused by the permanent death of brain cells that cannot be regenerated.

Finally, arteriosclerotic brain disease or strokes are more common among the elderly. Their onset is sudden, with people experiencing some loss in their intellectual and neurological functioning. For example, a man who suffers a stroke may experience weakness or paralysis on one side of his body. He may also lose sensation in his face and limbs. Immediate medical intervention and an aggressive rehabilitation program of physical therapy allow for the greatest improvement of the cognitive and neurological losses that result from a stroke.

The attitude of Church ministers and their determination to remain active plays a significant role in their ability to deal with any health impairment. Growing older, they also need a reasonably stable, familiar, and supportive living situation in order to continue functioning at an optimal level. As the number of elderly priests, sisters, and brothers increases, planning healthy and realistic living arrangements for them is of great concern to Church leaders. Helping older Church ministers make a decision to move from their present quarters to more appropriate ones is also of increasing importance. Today, we need to be realistic and creative in planning living situations for the final years of life. Past models of care for older religious and priests are often unsuitable for the present changed circumstances. Religious professionals of all ages need to be willing to involve themselves in developing new models. Dioceses and religious orders and congregations can share expertise and contain costs by working together on some living ventures. Such an approach would also reduce the duplication of services and allow for a greater variety of available living situations for older priests, sisters, and brothers. Among the many factors that will determine the specifics of suitable living arrangements for older Church ministers are the age and health of the group's members, their geographical distribution, available opportunities for limited ministry, and financial resources.

How can Church leaders be of help when the time comes for an elderly Church minister to move from a more active living situation to one more appropriate for the person's years and health? As with many other transitions, making this change calls for a chain of decision-making steps.[12] There are five of them and at each one various alternatives need to be evaluated. To begin with, this question needs to be asked: Must this move be made? Can this person continue to be maintained in his or her

12. Grateful acknowledgment is once again made to Naomi Golan, from whom this analysis is adapted (see *Passing through Transitions,* pp. 224-28).

present environment? Answering these questions can be the most difficult step in the process of helping the older person. The thought of moving frightens most of us. For many older people it is terrifying. An elderly pastor, for example, is overwhelmed by the bishop's request that he consider moving from the rectory to a retirement center for priests. This old man's memories and associations of his value and contributions to his Church are tied up with the physical attributes of his rectory, his garden, the streets of his neighborhood, and his parish. To leave them is, he fears, to suffer the loss of meaning in his life. First of all, then, one must help the individual determine if a move is necessary.

Second, if some change is called for then other living arrangements need to be investigated. Making a list of all possible options for living can be helpful. For some men and women religious these may include moving to a community with more support services such as a cook or people available for chaufferring them to appointments and activities. For others, it can mean relocating in a community with an elevator or in an infirmary setting with readily available nursing care and medical resources. Whatever living situation is chosen, it should be sensitive to the abilities and needs of the older person.

Third, after weighing alternatives, a choice needs to be made and ways of implementing it designed. Elderly people need to be prepared for any move they will make. Many need to sort out which possessions they will take with them and which will be left behind. This process becomes part of a mourning ritual and takes time. An elderly priest, for example, may give away many of his books and possessions when he moves to smaller quarters in a living situation with adequate nursing care. In leaving his present environment, he will probably spend time saying goodbye to old friends and parishioners, some of whom he may not see again.

Fourth, people need to be initiated into their new living situation. Consider the religious brother who moves into a large retirement community. He needs to situate his room in relation to the dining and community rooms and chapel. He must learn the customs and rules of the new community. It will also take time for this man to establish rapport with other community members, especially if they are drawn from several congregations.

When adjusting to their new residence, many older religious and priests experience anxiety and stress. One man is upset that the main meal is served at noon instead of at six in the evening as had been the custom in his previous residence. Another may become angry and confused as he tries to adjust to a new daily schedule.

Finally, as people become integrated into their new setting they go through a period of adjustment. As part of this process, some withdraw initially from others. They might spend more time sleeping than in the past. Others regress and make excessive demands for help even though they are not greatly incapacitated. Still others adapt well by channeling their energies into activities, attempting to overcome any handicaps, and finding new kinds of satisfaction within the realistic restrictions of their new environment. Accepting their own limitations, these men and women cope with their anxiety and loss by reaching out to others.

Living into late, late adulthood, people discover that it too is a time for conversion. There is a dying, a letting go of old self-images and understandings, but also a rising to new ones. As they lose loved ones to death, former roles, and even places of residence, many older Church ministers realize again that each of us enters the world alone and leaves it in much the same way. Death, closer than at midlife or even a few years ago, again causes some assessments to be made. The meaning of life is more apparent; the consequences of life decisions more clear. As they complete the work of the period, older priests and men and women religious, especially during the present age of transition, come to accept one of life's most significant learnings: at the heart of human psychological growth is Christianity's central paradox, the need to die in order to rise anew.

The years of adulthood, then, provide each of us with a series of alternating stable and transitional periods. During the stable periods we look toward our future; during the transitions we evaluate our past. The periods of transition give us an opportunity to rework important aspects of our life. During each one, for example, we can answer anew the question of personal identity. We can formulate who we are and where we are going in a way that is suitable for our age in life. In the following section I will discuss three areas that emerge and demand attention during every life transition: sexuality, spirituality, and fidelity. Finally, I will examine the topic of stress during the life cycle, discuss burnout, and suggest some practical ways to avoid it.

Part III:
Celibacy, Spirituality, Fidelity, and Change

Chapter Seven
Celibacy, spirituality and the life cycle

Today, committed celibacy is in trouble. The lives of many celibate Church ministers have lost their significance. More and more people are asking, "Why would anyone be celibate *now*—during the grand finale of the sexual revolution?" Even the small trickle of recent books heralding the "new celibacy" is looked on as something of a curiosity. One commentator dismissed the phenomenon as similar to going on a diet just when the banquet is being served.

To defend their celibate decision, a number of Church ministers reach uncomfortably for packaged answers: to be more available for ministry; to be free to love everyone and not just a single person; for the sake of the Kingdom. After a brave start, these initial attempts at explanation are often found wanting. Though New York's *Village Voice* reported in 1979 that the latest vogue was to "come out" as celibate, many priests, sisters, and brothers wonder if this commitment has a genuine place in their life. Admitting that celibacy has been a central part of Catholic tradition, some of these men and women question the relevance of committed celibacy during today's transitional age.

During times of life transition, these questions become more urgent. For example, a number of religious professionals, having made their formal life commitment at an early age, ask sincerely, "When I chose celibacy, did I really know what I was getting into? Did I know enough about sexuality and my own sexual identity to make an informed choice?" The answer is generally clear: no, they did not.

153

In recent years, sex has also fallen on hard times. Many people have discovered that sexual liberation does not automatically bring sexual fulfillment. In slaying some loathsome dragons, the sexual revolution created a number of new ones.[1] For example, replacing previous injunctions against masturbation are some equally strong directives that make masturbation something of a duty and, at times, equate its practice with therapy. In another example, Rollo May points out that during the Victorian age, "nice" men and women felt guilty if they experienced sex whereas today people feel guilty if they do not.[2]

In some circles, sex has been divorced from love, creation, romance, and intimacy. A number of men and women, with typical American practicality, work hard to "get good" at sex. For still others, sex is a commodity, something they "have." They have a car, they have dinner, maybe a swim, perhaps they even have the chicken pox, and they "have" sex.[3]

In attempting to view sex as a natural function integral to life, a number of leading sexologists insist that it should be removed from all ethical and social considerations. This removal trivializes people's erotic behavior by suggesting that it has little to do with anything else in their life.[4] As a consequence, sexual intercourse becomes a sport and is divorced from morality, responsibility, caring, compassion, and, at times, even common politeness.

More recently, a growing number of people have realized that sexual liberation divorced from love and creation is a reaction to past repression rather than the fruits of a hard-won revolution. They want to reclaim many of the qualities that made sex so precious in the past: intimacy, sympathy, the warmth of one-to-one relationships, and the sense of commitment. Seeing sex as

---

1. See George Leonard, "The End of Sex," *Esquire* 98, no. 6 (December 1982): 72.

2. See Rollo May, *Love and Will* (New York: W. W. Norton, 1969), p. 40.

3. See Leonard, "End of Sex," p. 74.

4. Ibid., p. 70.

one way of expressing care and love, these people have ceased to think of it as an aspect of their life that exists apart. Author George Leonard said it cogently: "Isn't it time we stopped thinking about sex and started thinking about something else? Like love?"[5]

Sex is a peculiar preoccupation of late-twentieth-century America. There can be little doubt that during the past few decades the United States has experienced a sexual revolution. This phenomenon has led to many positive results. Its influence is seen not only in changed behavior but also in the dramatic increase in available sexual information. Beginning with Alfred Kinsey's pioneering scientific studies of sexual behavior in men and women down through the more recent and well-publicized work of William Masters and Virginia Johnson, discussion about human sexuality has moved from offstage into the spotlight. A "knowledge explosion" has occurred in this area. However, rather than reminding people of their ignorance about the topic, the steady stream of information about sexuality has made many of them intellectually and emotionally arrogant. The fact of the matter is this: although we are much better off than fifty years ago, we still know relatively little about human sexuality.

Committed religious celibates, as well as everyone else, need knowledge about human sexuality. Equally important is some understanding of friendship and intimacy. Celibacy has often been separated from these important areas in the past. Today, committed celibacy among Church ministers is in trouble because it frequently does not communicate anything of significance. It is experiencing a real crisis of value and spirituality. Its meaning ambiguous, simple genital abstinence among Church ministers says little that is clear to most people. For example, in May 1978, the *New York Times* diagnosed the wave of "asexuality" that was sweeping the country as an antidote to traumatic sexual experiences such as divorce and the pain of casual sex. The lives of celibate men and women need to have significance for their commitment to make a public statement. However, if

---

5. Ibid.

celibate Church ministers lack values different from those espoused by their culture and a vibrant spirituality at the core of their commitment, people come to question the meaning and value of a celibate decision.

During a transitional time some difficult questions about celibacy need to be asked: What is committed celibacy? Can it be a meaningful and fulfilling choice during a time of transition? Can Church ministers committed to celibacy be sexually healthy and well adjusted or is celibacy to be equated with sexual repression? Are intimate and loving relationships incomplete without genital involvement? In this chapter, I will consider some of these questions, looking first at the many faces of celibacy and exploring some common misunderstandings about this way of life. I will then examine its development over the course of the adult years, especially with regard to the spiritual life.

The many faces of celibacy

Is there any simple way to explain why some people choose a life of committed celibacy? Probably not. A number of men and women decide on celibacy so as to grow personally, interpersonally, and spiritually; others do so because of their fear of sexuality; still others choose celibacy with little understanding of what it will entail. For those choosing wisely, celibacy teaches a great many lessons over the course of the life cycle, lessons about sexuality, the mystery of life, and relationships with other people and God. Stated simply, for people called to committed celibacy, their choice enables them to grow and mature in ways that another life decision would not.

There are many misunderstandings about celibacy. To begin with, committed celibacy is a foe of neither sexuality nor genitality. Although celibate love is not genital love, neither is it primarily genital abstinence. People can abstain from genital love and still not be celibate. Instead, committed celibacy is a personal and unique way of being sexual. Men and women who choose celibacy place their efforts on forms of love other than genital love.

Another misunderstanding is the confusion of celibacy with asexuality. The two states are quite different. In part, the confusion may arise from the fact that some Church ministers professing committed celibacy appear to be asexual. After talking with them, one is unsure whether the sisters, priests, or brothers are sexual persons. They appear sterile, rigid, and lack warmth and sensuality. These unfortunate characteristics can result from several factors: a poorly developed sexual identity, a fear of sexuality, the defensive use of a professional role, or a degree of sexual immaturity. People's asexuality, however, should not be blamed on their committed celibacy.

Sometimes celibacy is confused with discipline. Celibacy, however, needs to be a free choice. For a number of today's Church ministers, though, it is not. Meant to be a charism, celibacy has become a discipline. The results of this unfortunate development are like those of marriages that are coerced or arranged: they create more problems than they solve. Set up by the families of two people for reasons other than the development of a loving relationship between the couple, marriages such as these present built-in difficulties. In time, the man and woman may come to love each other. However, the marriage runs at least an equal chance of becoming merely functional.

Consider an unmarried teen-aged woman who discovers that she is pregnant. Both her family and that of her boyfriend pressure the couple to get married. They point out the importance of the child's having a name, and the family's need to be spared any embarrassment in this situation. If the couple marry, they *may* grow in love. However, the failure of many marriages entered into under these conditions suggests otherwise. Both parties may begin to look elsewhere for affection, support, and their challenge to grow. The marriage itself becomes functional. In time, the partners may resent each other.

Today a similar situation exists for some Church ministers. Although called to a particular ministry, they do not have the charism of celibacy. Certain ministries, however, have by Church law come to require a celibate commitment. For those without the charism who choose such a ministry, celibacy automatically becomes a discipline.

Discipline is a necessary ingredient for fully living out any Christian commitment.[6] Maturity always includes self-discipline. This quality contributes to the growth of people on a daily basis. Everyone needs discipline to live a life that is wholesome, satisfying, integrated, purposeful, and productive. For example, the young dancer exercises the discipline of regular practice in order to dance well, and scholars develop disciplined research skills so as to contribute to their area of interest. Physical health requires careful diet, physical exercise, and regular sleep. For some men and women, emotional growth calls for the disciplined rhythm of weekly psychotherapy sessions. In the spiritual life the discipline of regular spiritual direction as well as abstinence, fasting, meditation, and regular prayer plays a vital role.

If pursued as an end in itself, however, discipline becomes destructive and often gives rise to aberrations in behavior. Fasting and self-denial, for example, can become sources of pride rather than growth-producing ascetical practices. Discipline is excessive if it enhances one dimension of a person while harming another. No matter how spiritual the goal, a discipline that destroys a person's physical, psychological, or spiritual health is destructive and needs reexamination.

Men and women who accept their call to genuine celibacy need to practice discipline to live out this decision. This requirement is also true for anyone trying to live a committed Christian life. However, for these men and women, the discipline they practice is self-imposed, interior, and personal. Their self-discipline, far from being a destructive force, fosters growth. It is undertaken in the service of their life values. As such, it is also

---

6. For additional discussion of discipline and its role in the celibate and spiritual life, see Donald Goergen, *The Sexual Celibate* (New York: Seabury, 1974), pp. 214-17.

genuine asceticism. "Asceticism is a striving for the freedom of an authentic Christian life."[7] If a discipline is authentic asceticism, it will foster growth, enliven one's spiritual life, and increase one's awareness of the vital issues of the age. Contemporary asceticism needs to help individuals grow into the person they were meant to be and not mold them into some unrealistic and unattainable external ideal.

Today, some Church ministers professing committed celibacy, but lacking the charism, feel trapped. Genuinely called to a particular ministry, they feel forced to make compromises between their public commitment to celibacy and the personal living out of that commitment. In this age of transition, Catholics have been given an opportunity to examine the relationship between some Church ministries and celibate commitments. To address this issue honestly, they need to redefine ministry and understand the many dimensions of celibacy. Committed celibacy has lost its significance and spiritual roots because for many people it has become merely functional. The situation calls for some needed examinations and change.

A transition will take place when committed celibacy is separated from some Church ministries. People will experience a loss of the familiar, a period of darkness and exploration, but finally a new beginning. At that time, both ministry and committed celibacy will achieve their proper place among the People of God.

Finally, one's choice for celibacy is a decision to experience life in a way quite different from most people. The majority of other people are coupled; celibates are not. Coming from the Latin word meaning alone, celibacy is a positive choosing of solitude. Men and women professing celibacy do this because for them it is the best way to grow. Drawing an analogy between celibacy and vegetarianism will clarify some of these points.

---

7. Dan McGuire, *Thomas Merton on the Future of Monasticism* (Dubuque: Aquinas Institute of Theology Library, 1973, unpublished thesis), p. 10.

A vegetarian is not a person who detests meat, someone who avoids eating it because the taste is repulsive.[8] Instead, vegetarians are motivated not to eat meat for reasons other than a dislike for it. They choose vegetarianism even though it means they will not fit into their society's culturally accepted way of life. Stated simply, vegetarians choose an ascetical life-style in order to experience some aspects of life differently from the majority of other people.

Such a decision has many immediate results. For example, when dining out vegetarians remind others and are reminded themselves of their difference. Many others eat meat, they do not. People are curious about vegetarians and will question them about their choice and its consequences. Also, some men and women may be threatened by people who choose vegetarianism because they are different. These people may ridicule the choice to abstain from meat or dismiss it as an eccentricity.

Celibates have much in common with vegetarians. Because of their celibate decision, they experience the world differently from the majority of other men and women. Celibates have friends, acquaintances, even intimate relationships, but they are also alone in a way that is qualitatively different from people who are coupled. Committed celibacy reminds us that we enter the world alone, experience many periods of solitude throughout life's journey, and leave the world alone. Regardless of how close we come to another person, there is always part of each of us that remains unknown. This is our genuine mystery. For most people their aloneness hits home about midlife. This awareness is often behind the frantic question, "What have I done with my life now that it is half over?" For both the celibate and the midlifer, solitude enables them to face themselves and consider their limits. Moving from life's morning to afternoon, people begin to realize that celibacy and aspects of the cycle of life deliver the same message: solitude is important for growth.

Reminding people of their solitude, then, committed celibacy focuses men and women on their interior life and provides the

---

8. Goergen develops this example in some detail in *The Sexual Celibate,* p. 135.

possibility for growth in this area. With this understanding, there are some celibate persons, even those who are virgins, who fail to practice committed celibacy. Focusing too much attention on sexual abstinence and concerned about the narrow keeping of vows and promises, these men and women become self-involved. Their celibacy isolates them. In reality, celibacy is violated when people live their life without significance or spirituality. A transgression against a vow or promise of celibacy can be understood more readily than a committed life lived without meaning.

Committed celibacy and the life cycle

People are not born into committed celibacy, but rather grow and mature in their understanding of it. Seminarians and novices often get their first notions about celibacy from one person: the rector or novitiate director. A few Church ministers do not grow beyond this early and, at times, narrow concept of committed celibacy. Uncomfortable about their own sexuality, they accept someone else's understanding of celibacy rather than struggle to find their own. This situation is similar to eating a meal but not digesting the food. The result is discomfort and indigestion. Initial understandings about celibacy need to be tested out, developed, and changed over the course of the life cycle. Church ministers cannot be celibate at thirty-five and fifty-five in exactly the same way they were at twenty-five.

During novice adulthood, a number of priests, brothers, and sisters come to love another person deeply for the first time. Far from a passing infatuation, their feelings of love cause them to question their life commitment and choice of celibacy. For some Church ministers, a sexual awakening accompanies their experience of deep love. They become aware for the first time of the full force and power of their sexuality. As a consequence, past understandings of celibacy are called into question. Some Church ministers realize that they can be effective apostles without committed celibacy. Others fear missing the beauty of a loving relationship in their life. Still others become aware that one path to a loving relationship with God is through a deep, caring, and intimate relationship with another person.

Church ministers experiencing their first deep and loving relationship need to depend upon their fellow ministers for understanding and support. Sometimes both responses are lacking. Instead, there is suspicion and misunderstanding. The deep and loving relationship that a sister, brother, or priest develops with another person can frighten a number of their fellow priests and religious. These men and women may view being in love as the first step toward resigning from the priesthood, or seeking dispensation from vows. Rather than helping people face the challenge of their sexual awakening and new relationship, some sisters, brothers, and priests isolate their fellow ministers. They dismiss them with the conclusion that the loving partners will probably leave and get married. Such judgments can become self-fulfilling prophecies.

When the loving relationship is between two men or two women, the degree of fear and suspicion often intensifies. Again, rather than assisting people with their sexual awakening so as to help them understand, accept, and integrate their sexual feelings and identity, people often respond defensively and isolate those involved. In general, men and women, celibate and otherwise, need to be aware and accepting of their sexual feelings, both heterosexual and homosexual. When people keep important aspects of themselves out of their awareness, they miss an opportunity to become integrated men and women.

Because of American society's tendency toward homophobia and moral injunctions, and the psychiatric community's past misunderstanding of homosexuality, a number of men and women with a homosexual orientation do not begin to fully accept and integrate their sexual identity until late in novice adulthood. This situation is also true for many homosexually oriented priests, sisters, and brothers. Their task is often made more difficult by the homophobic fears present in some religious congregations and among other Church ministers. A supportive and understanding environment is necessary for people to grow in understanding, acceptance, and integration of their sexual orientation, be it homosexual or heterosexual. Also, sexual orientation is not a relevant criterion for deciding one's suitability to

live a priestly or religious life. Instead, one's willingness to attempt to grow into a life of committed celibacy that is rooted in
spirituality and has some significance is a better guideline.

During novice adulthood, then, one challenge people face is
their reworking of initial understandings about committed celibacy in the light of the period's experience. Especially about age
thirty, a number of Church ministers develop a deep and loving
relationship that forces them to question the meaning of their
celibacy and their religious or priestly commitment. Accepting
this challenge and relying on the support of others, Church ministers emerge from the transition around age thirty with a different and vital understanding of their sexuality, sexual identity,
and the place of deep, caring, and intimate relationships in their
life.

Mourning the loss of their wish for a family of their own is a
second challenge that some priests, sisters, and brothers face
during novice adulthood. Parenting children is a task of early
adulthood. Many couples give birth to a family during their
twenties and early thirties, and complete child rearing by their
midforties. With the number of women working outside the
home increasing steadily, this pattern has seen some recent adjustment as some women wait until their early thirties to begin
bearing children.

About the age-thirty transition, a number of Church ministers
committed to celibacy begin to have second thoughts about not
having a family, for a biological family of one's own is a concrete legacy for the early adult. Sisters, brothers, and priests as
they turn thirty are more aware that many of their contemporaries are forming families and mothering and fathering children.
As a result, some of the consequences of their earlier celibate
commitment begin to unfold.

The loss of forming a family of one's own needs to be accepted and mourned. Some people cope, instead, by using denial. They insist that there is still time left to parent children
should they change their life commitment. Others feel cheated
and become angry and critical of the shortcomings and inadequacies of their fellow ministers. To embrace the loss of parent-
hood, however, is to accept a limit that has resulted from an

earlier life decision. In accepting this limit and mourning the loss it entails, Church ministers are able to redirect their creative and nurturing parenting energy into other areas of life. If they refuse to grieve, then their parenting power remains trapped within them.

Finally, about age thirty a number of religious professionals develop a new understanding of their committed celibacy. This change requires being true to their lived experience, as well as having broader knowledge of emotional and psychological development, morality, and interpersonal relationships. The transition at midlife provides the next intense period of reassessment of their celibate commitment.

With the consequences of a celibate commitment even more apparent, the transition about age forty can be a difficult one for many Church ministers. However, the period also provides one with an opportunity to realize the fruits of committed celibacy. If the charism of celibacy is genuine and has been lived out sincerely, the rewards are great: self-knowledge, self-acceptance, appreciation of one's solitude and individuality, intimacy with others and God, and purpose in life.

At midlife, many Church ministers realize that without roots in the spiritual life, committed celibacy loses its meaning. The spiritual life needs to be at the core of genuine celibate living. As a result, not until they have discovered what it means to be a spiritual person will men and women called to celibacy feel at home with their choice. Consider a woman religious who spent most of her early life in ministry involved with a number of distracting activities. Burning the candle at both ends, she forced certain aspects of her life—friends, leisure, spirituality—into second place. Quite effective in ministry, her celibacy became more functional than anything else. Although successful, this woman begins to realize about midlife that her years of novice adulthood have been controlled by the tyrant of diversion. Wondering what she has done with her life, she remembers the wisdom of Oscar Wilde's comment: "The gods have two ways of dealing harshly with us: the first is to deny us our dreams, and the second is to grant them." During her transition, she is forced to face herself, the significance of her life, and the meaning of her celibacy. All are strangers to her. Her solitude, if embraced, will introduce her to these fellow travelers.

Solitude allows people to discover obscure forces within themselves. Church ministers who fail to be alone escape knowledge of those conflicts buried deep within them, conflicts they feel incapable of untangling or even touching. Solitude is a terrible trial. It cracks open and bursts apart the shell of our superficial securities.[9]

Solitude, though, also creates an eloquent language. It allows us to communicate with ourselves, others, and God. During the transition about midlife, the spiritual life is enriched by solitude; within the quiet, believers hear the Spirit of God. There are some experiences in life for which silence is the most appropriate language. To approach these times with the denotive, logical analysis common to the linguistic channel of communication is akin to translating poetry into prose—the words lose their meaning.[10] Sexual and mystical union are two experiences wherein silence is eloquent. At midlife, silence and solitude paradoxically become the most social forms of communication within the spiritual life. They bring us in touch with ourselves, others, and our God. For those who have grown into committed celibacy, this learning is something they have known from the beginning.

Moving into middle adulthood, people need to mourn their losses. At this time it becomes more apparent that in making some decisions early in life, in reality many others were also made. In choosing to grow through a celibate commitment, people chose not to grow through some other life decision. The lack of children or a spouse or lover needs to be faced by midlife celibate Church ministers. By grieving their losses they move into middle adulthood with new energy to mentor.

---

9. See Louis Bouyer, *The Spirituality of the New Testament and the Fathers,* vol. 1 of *A History of Christian Spirituality* (New York: Desclee, 1963), p. 313.

10. See Neil R. Castronovo, "The Realm of Relationship: When Words Are Not Enough," in Sammon, *Relationships,* p. 53.

Celibacy and a wish for immortality also become companions at midlife. About age forty, people experience the loss of their youth as early adulthood's illusory hero or heroine dies. They also have a powerful urge to leave an immortalizing legacy, to be remembered by future generations. Men and women choosing marriage and family early in life often hope that their children will insure their immortality. At midlife, they realize that this is just not possible. No other person can insure one's immortality. Children, for example, mature, move out on their own, and start a new life. Career and ministry also come to be found wanting. Goals have been achieved or one's falling short of them faced. The movement of the transition turns people toward life's meaning, their early Dream, and the interior life. By dwelling with these experiences for a while, celibate Church ministers come to discover the meaning of their life, values they wish to live by, and their possibilities for leaving a genuine legacy.

As people grow into late adulthood, their committed celibacy continues to develop. Regardless of the life path men and women take, in late adulthood it becomes apparent that people have more in common than not. Having lived the greater part of their lives, most individuals struggle with the same challenges: developing an interior life, assisting in the development of the Dreams of others, leaving a legacy. Why, then, one might ask, would a person choose committed celibacy if its goal is the same as any other life choice? Why face the difficulties and challenges of this committed life-style? What makes the celibate choice different from others? The answer is clear: for some men and women a life of committed celibacy is the best way to grow. Had the few called to it chosen another life they might have missed becoming the person they are now. Their lives of committed celibacy have relevance because they make visible a system of values and a way of life that appeals to both the deepest and the highest dimensions of human experience.[11]

11. For further discussion of sexuality and celibacy see Bishops' Commission on Priestly Life and Ministry, *A Reflection Guide on Human Sexuality and the Ordained Priesthood* (Washington, D.C.: U.S.C.C., 1983); and Robert Nugent, ed., *A Challenge to Love: Gay and Lesbian Catholics in the Church (New York: Crossroads, 1983).*

Chapter Eight

Transitions in faith and spirituality

What is faith?[1] Mark Twain said that it was "believing what any damn fool knows ain't so." Other people have come to a somewhat different conclusion. H. Richard Neibuhr, for example, sees faith as a search for unity and meaning in one's life, for that all-encompassing, stabilizing, and integrating center of value in which one can believe.[2] For some, faith means being caught up with "god values," those things of ultimate concern. Many midlife Church ministers ask these faith questions: "Who am I?" "For what causes, goals, and institutions am I pouring out my life, and what are my reasons for doing so?" "What are my most important hopes for my life and the lives of those I love?" "To whom or what am I committed in life, and in death?" Stated simply, these men and women are asking, "On whom or what do I set my heart?" Their answer to this question will determine the shape of their journey of faith.

Be they believers or nonbelievers, most men and women are concerned with faith and spirituality, with discovering what will make their life worth living. As part of this important search,

1. Grateful acknowledgment is made to James Fowler, upon whose writings most of the material in this chapter is based. For further discussion of faith and spiritual development, see Brewi and Brennan, *Mid-Life*; Fowler, *Stages of Faith*; James Fowler and Sam Keen, *Life Maps: Conversations on the Journey of Faith,* ed. Jerome Berryman (Waco, Tex.: Word Book Publishers, 1978); O'Collins, *The Second Journey*; and Helen Thompson, *Journey toward Wholeness* (Ramsey, N.J.: Paulist Press, 1982).

2. See James W. Fowler, *To See the Kingdom: The Theological Vision of H. Richard Niebuhr* (Nashville, Tenn.: Abingdon Press, 1974), chap. 5.

most people look for someone to love who in turn will love them, something they can value that will give them value, and something to honor and respect that also has the power to sustain them throughout their life.

What about faith and spirituality during an age of transition? Are they really possible? If so, what forms do they take, how do they develop, and how does the life cycle influence them? In this chapter I will address these important questions, first defining faith and spirituality, and identifying those factors that influence their early development. Next, I will look at our relationship to the real and false gods in whom we believe. Finally, I will examine the development of faith and spirituality over the course of the adult years.

Faith and spirituality: What are they?

Faith is not a noun but a verb. For a number of people, this is an unfamiliar notion. They associate faith with a body of beliefs, with content, and, most especially, with formal religion. Although faith plays an important role in each of these areas, it also transcends them. Beliefs or a creed, for example, spring from people's efforts to translate their experience of the transcendent into concepts or prescriptions. As a consequence, what faith sees is brought to expression. Religion is, in part, made up of those forms that faith creates for expressing, celebrating, and living in relationship with the transcendent. Faith, however, is the heart resting in a vision, not the mind giving intellectual assent to a blueprint.

The Latin word *credo*, usually translated "I believe," is, in reality, made up of two words: *cordia*, or "heart," and *do*, "to put, place, or give." According to this understanding, faith demands the giving of one's heart. In doing so, people begin to possess a quiet confidence and joy that allows them to feel at home in the universe. Living above a mundane level, they see, feel, and act in terms of a transcendent dimension. As a consequence, they find meaning in the world and their own life regardless of what may happen to them or to those they love.

Faith, then, rather than religion or belief, is at the core of the struggle to trust others and of the quest for meaning in life and a transcendent center of value and power. As such, it is an orientation of the total person and not just a separate part of life.

Spirituality has much in common with faith. It also is a life-giving and life-sustaining vision permeating and penetrating people's lives. Spirituality calls for symbols that embody and express that vision.

For Christians, there is but one spirituality: a call to discipleship in the Paschal Mystery, a baptismal spirituality; a call to conversion and intimacy with God. The process of conversion involves a "metanoia," a turning toward life.[3] The death and resurrection of the Paschal Mystery provide the means for this conversion. To "put on Christ Jesus," people first need to let go of their total way of making sense of things. Next, they must spend an extended period of time living with ambiguity and a deep sense of alienation. These "dark nights" are a necessary step on the road to conversion. As with any transition, there is eventually a new beginning. In the spiritual life, as elsewhere, this third stage of the transition cannot be forced. When men and women are ready to make a new beginning, they will find the means necessary.

Every period of life transition also offers the possibility of conversion. At the center of these times of reevaluation lies the spiritual question: "On whom or what do I set my heart?" People are given the opportunity not only for shaping their new period's life structure but also for finding new and enriching ways of being a disciple of the Lord.

Intimacy with God is another important aspect of the call to discipleship. The word "intimate" has at least two meanings. As an adjective, derived from the Latin *intime,* it means "intrinsic, innermost, and very personal and private." In contrast, used as a verb, intimate means to announce or make known. In the spiritual life both meanings apply. Being intimate with someone means coming to know the inner person, to uncover what is

---

3. Fran Ferder, F.S.P.A., and Rev. John L. Heagle point out that the opposite of "metanoia" is "paranoia," a turning away from life.

most essential. In the Old Testament such a process was tied up with a person's name: to know it was to possess the person. *Shem,* or "name," disclosed people's role in life and revealed something about the depth of their being. Stated simply, knowing someone's name gave access to the mystery of who the person was.

Moses wanted to know God's name. Having such knowledge meant penetrating the mystery of God and coming close to Yahweh. It implied intimacy. For Moses, however, and in the Old Testament in general, God was the somewhat distant "I am." In the New Testament, Jesus' God is the closer and more intimate *Abba,* Father. In part, then, intimacy is coming to know another's name.

The disciples described an intimate relationship with Jesus. In asking "Where do you live?" they were not just inquiring about the location of his home. Instead, they were asking, "What is your Dream? Can we come close, and will you let us know you?" The Lord's reply was, "Come and see." The word "come" can also have a number of meanings. One implies a journey as in "coming a distance." The journey of spiritual intimacy takes time and demands a growing relationship with God. These factors work against distance, the avoidance of depth, and not being known. In the final analysis, the spiritual journey invites people to an intimacy in which God can come close enough so they might be transformed.

Spirituality, then, is a call to intimacy, to discipleship, to embrace a life centered around Jesus and his gospel. In accepting this invitation, people also come to live out the second meaning of intimacy and make the Lord known by announcing that his news is indeed good.

How does faith develop?

The question "On whom or what is your heart set?" calls for people to reflect on the centers of meaning in their life. Such opportunities do not begin to present themselves until at least one's early twenties. Prior to this time, however, several factors work together and lay the foundation for a life of meaningful faith. With this notion in mind, one can say that faith begins during the earliest years of life and continues to develop throughout the life cycle. Faith unfolds gradually in the interaction between active, curious, and innovative people and their dynamic and changing environment. Early in life, several elements enhance the setting of one's heart on the transcendent. Among these are trust, the development of language, the principle of reciprocity, and the development of values.[4]

Trust is a necessary first ingredient for faith's development. At birth, people have a nascent ability to set their heart on someone or something of ultimate concern. Whether this capacity for faith grows and how it develops depend upon three factors: the manner in which children are welcomed into their world, those who receive them, and the environment that is provided. Taking form very early in life, faith grows out of people's experience with those who are close and care for them. Consider children born to parents who never really wanted them, or whose ambivalence about them was apparent. Any child will have a difficult time developing relationships of trust in such a world. Later in life the image of God as mother or father evokes memories of fear, distrust, and anger, rather than unconditional acceptance, warmth, and love.

As a result of their experiences, then, young children generally place or withhold confidence in those who care for them, their environment, and the larger world of meaning that begins to unfold. About this time also, people's first preimages of God have their origin. They are powerfully influenced by the child's ability or inability to trust others and the world.

With the development of language, a child's world changes dramatically. Reality begins to take on an episodic quality. Events appear somewhat like separate vignettes that are not necessarily part of a larger story. Consider young children's conversation. One animated comment of a three-year-old girl may not relate to any others she makes.

---

4. For additional information on child development, see any of the works of Jean Piaget, for example, *Play, Dreams, and Imagination in Childhood* (New York: Norton, 1962).

About this time also, children's experience of God and the meaning of their world is a collage of images given them by parents and other authorities, as well as their own history and the constructions of their imagination. There are many reasons for this. The first is that children are quite egocentric. Their ability to put themselves into the place of others and to see things from another's perspective is limited. As a consequence, most children are unable to compare two different points of view on the same subject. Instead, they assume their perspective represents the only available one.

In addition, young children do not fully understand cause-and-effect relationships. Being myopic, they focus on only one dimension of what has occurred. In part, this fact explains their assignment of partial and erroneous interpretations to many of the events in their world.

Finally, although the child's imagination is tremendously productive, it is also disorganized. Only with the later rise of more stable and self-reflective thinking will many of the long-lasting images formed during this period be sorted out. So, as yet unable to form their agglomeration of fragmented images into meaningful narratives, let alone step aside and reflect upon them, children move into middle and late childhood and continue their growth in faith.

Between the ages of approximately six and ten, boys and girls use stories to make sense of their experience. Reality's earlier episodic quality wanes. Children separate the real from the imaginary on the basis of their practical experience. If a child's world has been welcoming so far and has provided a place for the transcendent, anthropomorphic images of God also begin to emerge during this time. For example, God is "mother," "father," or "some benevolent person in heaven." God can also be "hurt," "pleased," "happy," "disappointed," "sad," and "angry."

Several factors explain the changes seen during this period. Children's ability to narrate their experience begins to give some coherence and unity to their world. In addition, many boys and girls learn to take the perspective of others, to see things from another's point of view. Their world begins to be built upon principles of mutual dependence and fairness. The notion of reciprocity also governs their relationship with God, as is evident in their prayer life. A fourth grader, for example, may bargain with God, agreeing to say so many prayers so as to pass an important examination. There is a magical quality to this pact. Although the values of fairness and reciprocity are seen most especially in the prayers of children, they are not entirely absent from those of adults. Theologian James Fowler provides a clear example of this situation in his report of a faith interview with a woman in her fifties, the mother of seven grown children. Describing a talk given by one of her parish priests, a man she admires and whose approach to religion she appreciates, this woman comments:

> Well I tell you now, last week he was saying that it was Advent and that, you know, just do one good thing, he said, for someone—just one this week. Some kind of thing—hold a door for someone that doesn't expect it. Just one little thing, and offer it up. Y'know, 'n this is what, this is what I find I need, you know. Sometimes you keep doing big things; you think, oh I have to say a whole rosary or any—to say a whole thing. Now I have a little picture of the Pope—oh, I have great faith in him, that Pope—Pope John—and over my sink I have a picture of him, and every day I say a Our Father, a Hail Mary, and a Glory Be to God. *And then when I need it, it's in the bank.* And now I have my children doing it, when they're walking to class and all, I say, "Build up your bank account." And when you sit in that dentist's chair and it goes, "Oooh!" You just say, "open the bank" and out it pours, and it works. . . . Well, it, you just know that if you get in a mess, you have that bank and it will open up and it will help you through the mess.[5]

Later in the same interview this woman describes her son Tom's relationship with God. In many ways it is like her own.

> Now I thought that one of the greatest things was Tom [one of her sons]. He decided, you know, that this going to mass was

---

5. Fowler, *Stages of Faith*, pp. 146-47.

too much and all. And then, oh that draft came along for Mack [another of her sons], and then it came along for himself. And he said, "You know, Mother, I go to church every Sunday now because I felt I can't be asking for a big favor and then not showing up. And then when something else happens," he said, "so it's easier for me to make a little effort each week."[6]

Some of the features of the faith life of this woman and her son, then, have their roots in the world of middle and late childhood where understandings of God and the world are based upon justice, reciprocity, and coherent and unifying stories.

As children grow into adolescence, they become more sensitive to the expectations and judgments of others. The early teen years are often a time of conformity wherein one's shaky adolescent identity interferes with the formation of independent perspectives. Images of the transcendent that portray a personal God are attractive to people during this period of doubt, insecurity, and fear of rejection. Many adolescent conversion experiences find their source in young people's hunger for a God who will know, accept, and confirm them deeply. The transcendent becomes a friend, companion, and comforter.

By this point in their development, people are aware of holding certain values. Most often they are similar to those of parents and other authorities. Although they articulate and defend these emotionally invested centers of meaning, young people have not yet made them the object of scrutiny. Philosopher George Santayana summarized the situation cogently. "We cannot know who discovered water," he said, "but we can be sure it was not the fish."[7] Living with unexamined values and a tacit system of meaning, early adolescents are in the same tank as the fish.

At times, values from the many areas of an adolescent's world come into conflict. The teen-agers' failure to examine their centers of meaning critically becomes evident in these situations. Consider a conflict between parental and peer values. The

6. Ibid., p. 147.
7. Ibid., p. 161.

discrepancy is generally resolved in one of two ways: compart-mentalization or creating a hierarchy of authority.[8] Using the first solution, the young person decides to act one way when with peers and another way in the presence of parents. In solving the dilemma with a hierarchy of authority, a teen-aged boy or girl might judge that peers and their values are most important and subordinate other authorities to them.

Adolescents, then, structure their world in interpersonal terms. Although they hold certain values, young people have had little occasion to step aside and examine them systemati-cally. Even so, their identity and early Dream can begin to take shape out of these centers of meaning.

As they mature into adulthood, a number of people begin to question their way of making sense of their world and take per-sonal responsibility for their values. Others, though, resist this transition. Rather than seeking meaning internally, they appeal to external authority to provide it. They also reaffirm their val-ues without first examining them. Feeling like fish out of water, these men and women cannot get back into the tank soon enough. Others, however, accept the invitation to question and thus create the possibility of formulating an initial answer to the spiritual question of whom or what their heart is set upon.

Gods: Real and imagined

People's commitments, in part, answer the question: On whom or what do you set your heart? Be they to a relationship, cause, institution, or value, commitments are centers of passion and energy that disclose men's and women's "god values." Sometimes, though, a stated commitment and a private style of life are at odds. Consider Church ministers who publicly profess interest in their spiritual life yet instead deify work. Insisting that the many demands of ministry come first, these men and women leave little time for the leisure and reflection necessary for the development of some aspects of their spiritual life.

---

8. See Fowler and Keen, *Life Maps*, p. 61.

Writing an obituary can help people determine their centers of value and power in life.[9] Such an accounting can also be a real eye-opener. Suppose for a moment that you had sudden heart failure or met with a freak and fatal accident. Your life is all over. Whatever you have done is the you that goes down in the history books, and everything that you planned on doing vanishes with the mind that considered it. Imagine that you are a fellow priest, community member, or friend who has taken on the task of writing an obituary for the diocesan newspaper or province notes. What would you write about yourself? Consider the things you did and did not do with the time given you. On whom or what was your heart set? Was it work, money, or a relationship? Perhaps you valued being admired and liked more than anything else. Maybe you found your treasure in being of service and caring about others. Then again, you might have given your life to maintain an institution, or to fight injustice. Whatever you built your life around, was it in keeping with your early Dream? Also, was it really worth all those years?

Commitments also reveal one's pattern of faith and shape a person's identity. Throughout the life cycle, people can exhibit several patterns of faith. Fowler identifies three: polytheism, henotheism, and monotheism.[10] Men and women living out the first pattern lack a center of value of sufficient transcendence to focus and order their life. Although interested in many minor "god values," they are without one compelling enough to unify their hopes and strivings. Consider the man with a polytheistic pattern of faith. Insisting that he should experience everything he desires, own everything he wants, and relate intensely with whomever he wishes, this man never brings all of his energy and passion to any value commitment or relationship in his life. Instead, he is detached in his approach to life and provisional about his commitments. Wanting it all, he often ends up with

9. This idea was first suggested in another context by William Bridges in *Transitions,* p. 126.

10. For a full description of these notions, see Fowler, *Stages of Faith,* pp. 19-23.

nothing of value. This man's identity also appears diffuse. Eventually no one, not even himself, knows who he really is.

Those men and women who withhold commitments throughout novice adulthood run the risk of taking up a polytheistic pattern of faith. Although it is important to explore options for living, a danger exists that the search will eventually become a defense against accepting limits and choosing a center of value that is also worthy of ultimate concern.

Protean polytheism is a variation on the polytheistic theme. People with this pattern of faith make a series of intense but transient commitments. As a consequence, they also lack a stable valued center that helps focus their life.

Men and women with a henotheistic faith pattern make intense commitments and build their life around a center of value and power. Their god, though, is an idol. Building their life around power, money, institutions, or projects of self-aggrandizement, henotheistic people invest deeply in a center of value that is unworthy of ultimate concern. Developing this pattern of faith is a danger for early committers. Men and women who made their central life choices during their transition into early adulthood may look to a relationship, religious congregation, style of life, institution, or a number of other "minor gods" to provide their life with meaning. During times of life transition they may be unwilling to surrender these idols so as to set their heart upon the real God. In part, their resistance may be due to the fact that their identity is also tied up with their early life choices. They fear that in the process of reexamining and reworking these choices they will lose their identity. However, only by surrendering to the loss and darkness of transitional times can they hope to make a new beginning in faith.

Today, in a number of dioceses and religious congregations, henotheism is also alive in what, at first glance, looks deceptively like a noble endeavor. Centering their lives around institutions and workaholism, a number of priests, sisters, and brothers are doing little more than worshiping new tribal gods. To some extent, their efforts may be an attempt to insure their immortality through institutions and thus avoid death, the central power that everyone must deal with in life.

The identity of henotheistic men and women is shaped by the gods they choose. For example, John Dean's search for power shaped his values and choices during the Watergate scandal. His henotheistic god eventually collapsed. Dislocated, Dean experienced pain and despair. This crisis also presented him with a transition and the opportunity for transformation. A number of Church ministers can identify with Dean's plight. In the current age of transition, a style of life with many of its trusted gods has collapsed. There is pain, anger, and some despair. The new center of value emerging from a period of darkness and exploration may look initially like an enemy and be held responsible for the death of previous forms of Church and religious and priestly life. It is, however, only with the death of these previous forms that new and more adequate ones can arise.

The monotheistic pattern of faith has a center of value and power that merits ultimate concern. Rather than investing in finite causes and institutions, monotheistic people place their trust and loyalty in the transcendent. In doing so, these men and women do not overlook centers of value that are less universal and transcendent. Instead, they place them in an order of priority. Paradoxically, such an ordering brings balance to Church ministers' lives. By placing their primary center of meaning and value in the transcendent and immanent God, lesser gods such as prayer forms, ministry, leisure, and many other aspects of life fall into place. Monotheistic faith, then, assures that one's god will not be a building, a finite cause, or an extension of some conscious or unconscious need, but rather of ultimate concern.

For many men and women, midlife provides the best opportunity for the development of a genuine monotheistic pattern of faith. Faced with limited time in life and questions about the meaning of the last four or so decades of their existence, people are eager to center their lives around someone or something of ultimate value.

The structures and values of the communities to which people belong also shape their pattern of faith. An interactional process takes place again between active and innovative men and women and their dynamic and developing environment. Thus, not only can individuals be henotheistic, but entire groups may take on this pattern of faith. Rather than centering their life on the real God, these groups may worship at the altar of institutions, success, traditions, styles of dress and life, prayer forms, and other potential idols. For both individuals and communities, growth in faith and the spiritual life results from challenges to their existence, life crises, and the disruption of "business as usual." Some theologians call these events revelation. Whenever people or communities experience disequilibrium and change they are also called to new patterns of faith and spirituality. Life transitions provide one arena in which to examine these invitations.

Faith, spirituality, and the adult years

The adult years provide a number of opportunities for transitions in faith and spirituality.[11] The question of whom or what one's heart is set upon can be answered more clearly as a person grows older.

About the early twenties, many people start to throw off their dependence upon others for the construction and maintenance of their identity and pattern of faith. Stated simply, they ask more serious and penetrating questions about the meaning of their life. This work is carried out in conjunction with several other tasks suitable to the period. A number of men and women, for example, leave home and begin to establish their first provisional life structure. As they become more autonomous so does their faith. Authority also comes to be found within oneself.

During novice adulthood, then, people develop their ability to stand alone, become reflective, and form an ideology and independent outlook. As part of these efforts, many also question their center of meaning and value. They need to stand alone and examine their pattern of faith. Consequently, religious symbols and rituals, formerly understood as mediating the sacred in direct ways and therefore sacred in themselves, are questioned. Examining a liturgical ritual or religious symbol, for example,

---

11. Once again, I gratefully acknowledge James Fowler, upon whose work this analysis is built. He should not, of course, be held responsible for some of my conclusions.

the novice adult often concludes that it does not *mean* anything. For a symbol or ritual to be truly meaningful, these men and women protest, they should be able to translate its meaning into definitions, propositions, and conceptual formulations. Carrying out such a process results in gains and losses. Theologian Paul Tillich concluded that when a symbol is recognized as a symbol by those who relate to the transcendent through it, it becomes a broken symbol. A poignant example of this situation in novice adulthood is contained in a story about theologian and cultural analyst Harvey Cox. It concerns the loss of his primal naiveté about a central symbolic act for Christians: the Eucharist. During high school Cox, a Baptist, would often attend services with friends at the local Catholic church. A Catholic girl whom he was dating near the end of high school went off to college while he stayed home to finish his senior year. She came home for Christmas and together they attended a midnight Christmas Eve mass. As the congregation began to receive the Eucharist, Cox's girl friend, having just completed Anthropology 101, turned to him and whispered, "That's just a primitive totemic ritual, you know." Cox's reply was predictable. "A what?" he said. She replied with self-assurance, "A primitive totemic ritual. Almost all premodern religious and tribal groups have them. They are ceremonies where worshippers bind themselves together and to the power of the sacred by a cannibalistic act of ingesting the mana of the dead god." As one can imagine, communion was never quite the same again for Cox. When a symbol is recognized as such, it becomes a broken symbol.[12]

The ability to question and reflect upon one's center of value is an important developmental gain of novice adulthood. To form a genuine monotheistic faith and grow in discipleship to the Lord Jesus, Church ministers need to determine if the resting place of their heart is worthy of this ultimate concern. Reflection and interiority are the key to this knowledge. Although a number of men and women complete this task during early adulthood, the exploratory and externally oriented nature of the

12. See Fowler, *Stages of Faith,* pp. 180-81.

period hinders many others from doing so. Consequently, many people evaluate their pattern of faith for the first time during midlife.

By their early forties, most people have known some suffering, loss, grief, responsibility, failure, and defeat in life. They have also made permanent commitments of effort and energy. These facts set the stage for a serious evaluation of one's pattern of faith. A satisfactory answer to the spiritual question becomes more urgent. In the process, one's past needs to be reclaimed, elements of childhood's faith integrated, and the deeper voices of oneself heard. A woman religious, for example, who learned more mistrust than trust during her developing years now needs to look at the effect of her past on her relationships, self-image, and faith and spirituality. Another Church minister, burdened by the demands of responsibility too early in life, must be willing to assess the benefits and costs of this situation. His transition at midlife provides him with the opportunity to discover less duty-bound and more adventuresome and playful aspects of himself that can, ultimately, enrich his faith.

Spirituality and faith are evaluated with seriousness at midlife because one's life is probably half over. Contradictions between present reality and one's early Dream need to be brought to the surface and addressed. Perfect resolution, though, is not a necessity. Midlifers are better able to live with ambiguity, mystery, wonder, and apparent contradictions. Completing the work of the transition, a number of men and women find their faith richer and more life giving not only for themselves but also for others. Moving into middle adulthood, they are better able to mentor others in discipleship, having made the journey themselves.

Finally, some men and women undergo a transition in faith that leads them to become disciplined activists. Their feel for the transcendent gives their actions and words an extraordinary and compelling quality. As Christians, having seen the Lord, they pay little heed to self-preservation and institutional arrangements. The devotion of these men and women to justice and compassion will, at times, offend parochial structures. Consider

Martin Luther King. His "Letter from a Birmingham Jail" was not written to the sheriff or to the Ku Klux Klan, but to a group of moderate and liberal religious leaders who had pleaded with him to stop the pressure his followers were creating with their nonviolent demonstrations in the city. King's refusal to overlook the more blatant aspects of segregation undermined the compromises that many blacks and whites had made to accommodate themselves to a racist society.

Teresa of Calcutta is another example of a person transformed by a transition in faith. As a foreign-born woman religious in her late thirties she was the director of a girls' boarding school. Traveling to a retreat, she was overwhelmed by the number of abandoned people lying in the city streets and left to die. The not yet lifeless limbs of some of these forgotten people were already being gnawed by rodents. Confronted by these grim sights, Teresa felt a call to a new form of vocation—a ministry of presence, service, and care to the abandoned, the forgotten, the hopeless. In a world where poverty is a fact of life, where strategies of "triage" are advocated by writers and policymakers to insure that resources are not wasted on those who have no chance of survival and useful contribution, what could be less relevant than the ministry she planned: carrying these dying people into places of care, washing them, caring for their needs, and affirming by work and deed that they are loved and valued by God. But in a world that demands that people pull their own weight and says they have worth only if they contribute something of value, what could be *more* relevant than this work?[13]

Men and women whose faith transitions cause them to spend themselves to transform the present world into a transcendent reality are not more perfect than others, just more lucid, simple, and human. By its respect for life and endorsement of nonviolence, their leadership affronts the pragmatism of usual notions of justice and political change. Often enough, these men and women of mature faith are rejected by many of their contemporaries or killed.

---

13. Ibid., p. 203.

Faith and spirituality, then, do not remain stagnant over the course of the life cycle. To question seriously on whom or what one's heart is set is a normal and necessary task of adulthood. With each life transition we are presented with another opportunity for clarifying and deepening our answer. During these times our center of value, meaning in life, personal identity, and answer to the faith question get shaken up. We are also asked to give up our previous way of making sense of our world. Many men and women discover the Spirit's movement in their life and are able to hear the voice of their God in the quiet and solitude that come about from surrendering to the challenge of transitions.

Today's Church appears to be experiencing a crisis of faith. Asked again where their treasure lies, the People of God seek an ever more genuine and life-giving answer to this question.

Transitions in faith and spirituality are similar to others in life. First there is an ending, followed by an empty, fallow time, and finally a new beginning. The fears that accompany other transitions are also seen here. What will be lost? Will the future be as satisfying as the past? There is also grief over the loss of the familiar. It is well to remember, though, that at the core of transitions in faith and spirituality is the central belief of Christianity, the Paschal Mystery: we must die first in order to be reborn.

Chapter Nine

The virtue of fidelity in an age of transition

During an age of transition, is there any justification for something so total and seemingly irrevocable as a permanent commitment? Today the answer to this question appears in doubt. Consider the evidence about the "breaking" of permanent commitments. In 1974, 980,000 American marriages ended in divorce.[1] During the intervening years this number has increased dramatically. Some states report that divorce requests outnumber the petitions for marriage licenses. At the same time, priests, sisters, and brothers have been resigning from their dioceses and congregations in large numbers. Still other men and women are reluctant to enter into any lifelong commitment for fear that it will limit their freedom and interfere with their emotional and psychological development. Can anything be said in defense of permanent commitments during our present age of change, upheaval, and chaos? In this chapter I will discuss this important question.

In doing so, I will first define commitment, perseverance, and fidelity. Next, I will examine two critical aspects of fidelity: the Dream and responsibility to others. Finally, I will explore the practice of fidelity over the course of the adult years, focusing on why the breaking of a commitment, in and of itself, is no guarantee of growth.

---

1. Cited in John Haughey, *Should Anyone Say Forever?* (Garden City, N.Y.: Doubleday, 1975).

What is a commitment?

Every commitment is a choice that involves a promise.[2] People determine their personal, interpersonal, intellectual, spiritual, and occupational growth by making choices. They also develop their sense of self primarily by choosing. Stated simply, "putting down roots" is the best way to grow. Consider the young man who struggles with a decision between a career in medicine and a priestly vocation. His desire to minister to others motivates the man's attraction to these two life directions. In choosing one over the other, though, he decides to live out certain aspects of his personality and to neglect and inhibit others. Some people are lucky enough to be able to wed their many interests. Although ideal, this solution is just not possible for most men and women. Instead, they must make choices and over time try to enhance their lives and realize their potential within the limits of these choices. They must also bear the responsibilities and tolerate the costs of these decisions. More than anything else in life, the choices that men and women make define them and help them grow.

A promise is another important aspect of every commitment. A particular kind of choice, it describes something that one intends to do in the future. For example, a young woman promises to be poor, chaste, and obedient within the structure of a particular religious congregation. She is not making a prediction about her future. Instead, this woman is stating her firm intention. In making the promise, then, she is not merely describing her present state of mind but is binding herself to a future course of action. To make a promise is the surest way for people to determine the direction of their life rather than have it set for them.

---

2. Haughey provides an excellent discussion of commitment as a choice and a promise compatible with freedom in his *Should Anyone Say Forever?*

Commitments and freedom

At first glance, freedom and commitments appear incompatible. Failure to commit oneself, however, is no guarantee of greater freedom. Many people believe that their degree of happiness in life will be directly related to the number of options they have. Conventional wisdom suggests that to increase their freedom all men and women need do is increase their capacity for having their own way. George Gilder points out the fallacy of this belief. Writing in *Naked Nomads,* Gilder reports that depression, addiction, disease, disability, loneliness, poverty, and nightmares are the dirty sheets and unmade mornings of many swinging singles in America.[3]

There are many other sides to freedom. Knowledge of them is critical to any understanding of the relationship between freedom and commitment. First, freedom refers to the capacity of people to be self-determining. For example, men and women are free to decide where, or with whom, or under what circumstances they will "put down roots." Also, by promising to live out a particular style of life or relationship, people choose freely to grow in one direction and not another. Although it is important to explore, to experience different options, and to be an adolescent for a while, it is equally important to avoid being a lifelong adolescent. A number of people continue to explore throughout their lifetime, but perpetual adolescents use exploration to withhold themselves. Rather than living their life, they dabble in it.

Second, in making any commitment, freedom is not surrendered. In fact, it may be enhanced by a person's choices. For example, by committing himself to the priesthood a young man finds that his potential for psychological, apostolic, and spiritual growth is greatly enhanced. Possibilities for developing and using his talents increase, his capacity for intimacy grows, and his relationship with his God becomes deeper and more life sustaining. In contrast, people who insist on keeping all of their options open and refuse to commit themselves to anyone or anything can

3. George Gilder, *Naked Nomads* (New York: Quadrangle, 1974), pp. 8-21.

miss the opportunity for intimate relationships, meaningful work, and a sense of personal integrity in their life.

In summary, then, avoiding commitments can eventually lead to becoming unfree, to having one's life determined by outside forces. Commitment is a choice and involves a promise, but it is quite compatible with freedom.

Commitment and perseverance

Still another aspect of commitment is visible in today's world: the "breaking" of commitments. Early in life, a number of men and women commit themselves to values, God, and relationships with others. As their experience and understanding of themselves, each other, and their God change and grow, they try to live out these commitments faithfully. In the enthusiasm of early adulthood, people often make vows intended to be permanent. In the light of later years, however, they cannot always keep them.

The practice of fidelity as a virtue cannot be equated with the keeping of commitments. Perseverance can be a poor measure of fidelity. Sometimes a relationship dies or needs to be brought to an end. Clinging to commitments solely because they have been promised or vowed, persevering in them even though the results are poisoned relationships, destructiveness, and a lack of life, is an exercise in pseudocommitment rather than fidelity. The virtue of fidelity is exercised in change as well as stability.[4] There are times when fidelity to oneself, others, and God calls for an acknowledgment that a commitment has died.

This thought frightens many people. They resist any notion that threatens their life decisions. For example, many people react anxiously to recent statistics regarding divorce and resignations from religious and priestly life. They wonder fearfully, will life commitments survive as we have known them? Such fear interferes with their ability to examine the genuine place of commitments in their life. They need to befriend their anxiety so as

---

4. For an elaboration of this concept, see Whitehead and Whitehead, *Christian Life Patterns,* pp. 100-106.

to understand the role of commitments and the practice of the virtue of fidelity.

Ideally, commitments should reflect the deepest currents in people's lives, be a path to personal, interpersonal, and religious intimacy, and challenge them to grow. This is often not the case in either committed relationships or priestly and religious life. Motivations for making commitments vary, as does the ability of people to deal with the challenges of their particular life choices. Some men and women use their commitments in ways that were never intended: to avoid the pain of self-discovery or the search for a genuine identity. Still others ask their vocational choice to provide them with an identity and meaning in life. Rather than developing from them, their sense of self merges with their commitments.

For many men and women, then, making and maintaining commitments, in and of itself, fails to insure personal, interpersonal, and spiritual development. However, breaking a commitment is not necessarily indicative of growth. The making and breaking of commitments is not the primary issue in any discussion of fidelity. Instead, viewing fidelity as an attempt to live life with integrity and responsibility to others provides more fertile ground for discussion. A quick look at the plight of two midlife fictional characters will shed some light on this situation.

Fidelity: The Dream and responsibility to others

"Something must have happened to me sometime," Bobby Slocum tells us, "something happened to me that robbed me of confidence and courage and left me with a fear of discovery and a positive dread of everything unknown that may occur."[5] At midlife, Slocum confesses that he gets the "willies" when faced with a closed door. He assumes the worst: something horrible is happening behind it, something that will affect him adversely. With his life in turmoil, he complains about his children and unhappy wife, his perspiring hands, and his voice, which sounds strange to him. He wonders about the meaning of all these signs.

---

5. Heller, *Something Happened,* p. 6.

An examination of Slocum's life, his choices regarding work, marriage, and family, and his values and interests reveals that he fails to practice the virtue of fidelity. He is guilty on two counts. One, he is reluctant to be faithful to his Dream. Two, he refuses to give others any claim over himself or his life. Living without integrity, Slocum avoids creating any expectation in people about what he will do for, to, or with them.

In contrast, Eddie Anderson practices the virtue of fidelity.[6] With midlife struggles similar to Slocum's, this familiar fictional character comes to very different resolutions. Losing touch with his Greek heritage, becoming an advertising executive rather than a writer, marrying and forming friends to enhance his career, Anderson almost succeeds in choking his early Dream to death. At midlife, though, he struggles to return to its spirit, reworking it so that it revitalizes rather than tyrannizes his life. In doing so, Anderson is genuinely faithful. He makes his Dream a prominent feature of his existence and gives others a real claim over himself and his life.

The midlife journeys of Bobby Slocum and Eddie Anderson illustrate the following point: the practice of fidelity cannot always be equated with commitments or the keeping of commitments. Although Slocum is committed and perseveres, he is also self-involved and unfaithful to his unique and life-giving Dream. In contrast, Anderson, having broken his commitments by failing to persevere in his original life choices, is faithful to the deepest currents within himself and others. Faced with their transition at midlife, these two men make very different choices: Slocum allows his life to become constricted and fearful; Anderson deals with the pain and uncertainty of the "journey homeward to himself."

Fidelity as a virtue

In old English the word "virtue" meant an inherent strength, an active quality. At times it was used to describe the undiminished potency of well-preserved liquors and medicines. Fidelity

---

6. See Kazan, *The Arrangement.*

is a virtue. People who practice fidelity struggle to overcome the feeling of staleness that threatens any commitment to radical love lived out over time.[7] One important result of their efforts is an ability to sustain freely pledged loyalties in spite of the inevitable contradictions among value systems.[8] Two other components of the virtue are its personal or Dream aspect, and its interpersonal or relational feature.

When people fail to practice the virtue of fidelity, their lives lack an active and spirited quality. This was Bobby Slocum's dilemma.

Failing to develop the personal and interpersonal aspects of his commitments, Slocum ceased to practice the virtue of fidelity. He began to "walk through" his commitments and failed to be present to them.

Fidelity and the Dream

One's Dream is an important aspect of the practice of the virtue of fidelity. This vague sense of self-in-the-world emerges during the adolescent years and answers the question, "What shall I do with my adult life?"[9] Filled with illusion, the Dream is one's personal myth. In recalling their own adolescent years, people will remember fantasies of magnificent intellectual or athletic feats, or inspiring and sustaining visions of becoming the excellent teacher, the dedicated priest or nurse, the wife-mother in a particular kind of family, the highly respected member of one's community. Adolescents use fantasy to explore their world. They dream about the kind of life they want to live. At times, they fashion worlds they can never hope to attain: the would-be hero or heroine in pursuit of a noble quest.

---

7. See Sister Margaret A. Farley, "A Study of the Ethics of Commitment within the Context of Theories of Human Love and Temporality" (Ph.D. diss., Yale University, 1974).

8. See Erik Erikson, *Insight and Responsibility* (New York: W. W. Norton, 1964), p. 125.

9. For more information on the Dream, see chapters 4 and 5 of this book and Levinson, *Seasons of a Man's Life.*

In young adulthood, the Dream is fueled by omnipotent fantasies. This situation is necessary because at this time the possibility of accomplishing such a Dream is slight. Young adults need to believe they are greater than they actually are in order to accomplish all that is asked of them by themselves and others. Growing older, they make choices and commitments, give their Dream a definition, and find ways to live it out. In building their life around the Dream during early adult years, people give themselves a better chance for personal fulfillment.

In some ways, each Dream is similar to that of Martin Luther King in his 1963 "I Have a Dream" speech. King's Dream filled his listeners with a sense of excitement and vitality. When people begin to actualize their Dream in their life, the result is much the same. Whatever the nature of an individual's Dream, that person has the task of giving it greater definition and finding ways to live it out. Conscious commitments often make the Dream more explicit. They are external signs of internal currents in men's and women's lives.

Betrayal of one's Dream or an inability to give it a place in one's life leads to an impoverished existence, and gives rise to difficulties in later developmental periods during the adult years. Building a life around the Dream, though, does not negate the necessity of reworking it into one's life at midlife and during other developmental transitions. During these periods people sometimes have to deal with the illusion that the accomplishment of their Dream will in and of itself insure their living "happily ever after."

The midlife transition is an especially critical time for modifying the Dream, primarily because men and women realize quite clearly for the first time that they are going to die. As part of their midlife developmental work, people must be willing to understand and evaluate the place of the Dream in their life. Some Church ministers find that they have compromised their Dream, or that their pursuit of it is increasingly in conflict with another way of living.

Until midlife, people tend to minimize those aspects of themselves that are in conflict with their Dream. Doing so leads to illusions that must be confronted during the transition about age forty. Men and women must admit that some of their life goals may actually be in conflict with their Dream and that other people are not in the world solely to facilitate the realization of their personal Dream.

In undertaking this task of Dream evaluation, some midlifers are overwhelmed by the gap they find between their early ambitions and what they have in fact become. In order to bring personal commitments more into line with the spirit of one's Dream, a man or woman must reevaluate these commitments at midlife and also during every transitional period. *This task is a very necessary and normal part of adult development.* If people are unfaithful to their Dream, life will simply close in on them and bring to a halt their growth at the personal and interpersonal levels. The demands of duty will rankle more and more, and these people will endure the pressure they face only by encapsulating themselves in an isolated world of their own. They will become distant observers of what once was an important part of their life.

As part of their developmental work at midlife, men and women also need to free themselves from the adolescent tyranny of their Dream. They practice the virtue of fidelity by demythologizing their early Dream and mourning the losses that come with such a process.

Midlife fidelity, then, includes coming to terms with the gaps, contradictions, and illusions in one's life. The Dream will never be realized completely; the would-be hero or heroine will always have flaws; even in success one must accept partial failure. At midlife many people are surprised to find that when they no longer feel the need to be remarkable, they are at last able to be themselves. For midlifers practicing fidelity, this is a significant discovery. Their newly acquired sense of who they are and are not insures that the commitments they make or renew more truly reflect the deep inner currents that direct their lives.

Fidelity and identity

The practice of the virtue of fidelity is also linked closely to one's personal sense of identity. Identity answers the "Who am I?" question throughout life. In early adulthood, people resolve it by exploring their world, experiencing crises, and making choices. Some identities come cheaply, whereas others are purchased at great price. Some young people, for example, are highly committed but have failed to explore options for living or to allow themselves the experience of a crisis. Hence, they "foreclose" the process of identity achievement and make a premature decision about their personal identity. This foreclosure allows them to look away from the contradictions and ambiguities that lie within.

Those Church ministers who have achieved rather than foreclosed their identity are mature, able to care for others in a nonbinding and noncompulsive manner, and generally are not greatly concerned with personal conflicts. Because they have explored those alternatives available to them, these people have attitudes and positions that are not merely reflections of parental or community norms. They have resolved many authority issues and need less reassurance from their peers. Even though these men and women will have to rework their identity in response to the changes and developmental crises of their adult years, to a large extent their commitments reflect the inner direction of their lives.

Those who foreclose their identity, by contrast, are quite "well behaved." However, their commitments are often externally determined and are not integrated with the inner currents of their life. It is almost as though they have adopted someone else's Dream rather than engage in the struggle to come to know their own. The experience of change in their life threatens these men and women and seriously challenges their commitments. Because their commitments are often enough the sources of their identity rather than the products of a sense of who they are, these men and women resist any changes that might allow them to discover their own personal Dream. If they permit themselves the experience of change, crisis, and the discovery of their

Dream, people who have foreclosed their identity may on the one hand, have to change their commitments in order to be faithful to their newfound Dream. On the other hand, they may wish to recommit themselves in a new and vibrant way to their original promises after having found that those decisions still reflect the inner directions of their life.

People who have foreclosed their identity, then, are really pseudocommitted. They are avoiding the risk of personal search and self-discovery by asking the object of their commitment to provide them with an identity and sense of direction in life. For the man or woman with a foreclosed identity, what looks like the betrayal of a commitment is many times a long overdue withdrawal from an unhealthy pseudocommitment.

In summary, the Dream faces men and women toward a particular horizon; it points their life in a particular direction. When horizons shift, when men and women rework their Dream into their lives, new commitments frequently strain former commitments or cause them to be discarded. Ultimately, commitments must be brought into line with one's Dream. Eddie Anderson undertook this task so as to be able to live with greater integrity. If people believe honestly that God is revealed in their history, then the Dream is one touchstone that can be used to measure fidelity to God.

One's Dream begins in adolescence and grows and becomes more realistic with the developmental work of each transitional period. The more men and women integrate their Dream with their personal sense of identity, and the more their commitments reflect attributes of their Dream, the greater the possibilities for their personal, interpersonal, and spiritual fulfillment. It is always necessary, in fact imperative, that individuals question and reassess their commitments and the relationship of these commitments to their maturing Dream. People are free to pursue their Dream, to ratify and accept it, or to turn away and reject it.

Befriending, living out, and liberating oneself from the adolescent tyranny of the Dream are important tasks for the practice of the virtue of fidelity. There is, however, another aspect of fidelity that needs examination, the relational or interpersonal component.

Interpersonal aspect of fidelity

At times of transition, men and women need to rework aspects of their Dream into the fabric of their life. This process may entail changes in commitments or result in the deepening of present ones. However, people do not make decisions about their life commitments in isolation. Rather, their relationships are often the most important factor assisting them in this process. The practice of the virtue of fidelity needs to be affirmed by others. Thus, during this reworking process, people need to call upon others for assistance.

Because commitments are a natural way of expressing the love a person has for another and for God, an ideal preparation for commitment is the experience of intimacy. Commitments are also a way of proving and preserving love. For these reasons, in reworking one's Dream, fidelity requires that men and women consider those to whom they are already committed. These people have helped them to become what they already are; they have assisted with the development and maturation of the Dream.

Any life commitment makes individuals responsive to and also responsible for other people. Stated simply, in the lives of all of us there are significant men and women to whom we become responsible when we make any life decision. After that point, future decisions are not ours alone. Consider a married woman who is offered a position that will advance her career. Taking the new job, though, will also require relocating her family. This woman will not make her decision about the position in isolation. She needs to consider her other life commitments: her relationship with her husband, her children and their well-being, her friends and local involvements. Although the intrapersonal aspects of any life commitment are important, so also are the interpersonal ones.

When people feel that their state in life and Dream are incompatible, they do not necessarily need to change their present circumstances. Such a decision may be simple resistance to the pain required for growth. If a commitment is changed for this reason, people will find themselves facing the same difficulties in later commitments. They are using a geographical cure to cope with their transition rather than practicing fidelity. Some examination of permanent commitments will amplify these points.

Permanent commitments

Although everyone needs to be an adolescent for a while, all people eventually need to root themselves. Most men and women do not have a problem with commitments, but rather with the idea of permanence. However, there appears to be an intrinsic connection between "forever" and some commitments.[10]

The justification for a permanent commitment is simple: no better way to grow has been found. A permanent commitment enables people to give their life meaning. Such a promise, far from preventing human growth, fosters it. Any commitment, however, that intends permanence but fails to flow from or at least give the promise of leading to love will be a deterrent to real growth. A permanent commitment must always be judged in terms of the fruit it bears. If a man or woman becomes bored, passively indifferent, resentful, and confused in a permanent life commitment, one must wonder what source of life and vitality it provides.

A permanent commitment appears justified only when the object of one's commitment is consonant with fulfilling the transcendent end that one is capable of attaining. God and other people are the only objects of commitment that appear to qualify for this role. Commitments to institutions or ill-defined theoretical notions may eventually sap the life from any commitment. People who are fulfilled transcend themselves. The quickest way to get outside of oneself is to make oneself vulnerable to another person.

People express their love for another person by saying forever. This word, however, does not mean to persevere "come what may"; rather, it is an aspiration to *become together* "come

---

10. See Haughey, *Should Anyone Say Forever?*, p. 57.

what may." Forever, then, does not imply fixity. A permanent commitment is not once and forever. Every conscious rechoosing is a renewal of one's original commitment. In other words, the making of vows does not signify the journey's end, but heralds a journey well begun.

Some illustrations of the practice of fidelity

Examples of recent changes in religious congregations and the life of Mary illustrate several of the points developed in this chapter.

The Dream and allowing others some claim on oneself are two major aspects of the practice of fidelity. These two components are quite apparent in religious congregations that have historically survived critical periods of change and have entered into a period of community revitalization.[11] I have already pointed out that the dominant image of religious life has seen several shifts across the centuries. These shifts in emphasis reflected major changes in society and the Church.

Each major shift has been heralded by some significant new foundations that embodied the changed image of religious life in a striking manner. The Franciscans and the Dominicans, for example, divested themselves of landed wealth and thus gave new life to the image of evangelical poverty. Their witness stood in sharp contrast to the wealth of many of the existing monasteries. The foundation of these two communities heralded a shift from the age of monasticism to the age of the mendicant orders.

During any transition period some religious orders go out of existence. The ones that survive manage to blend the new dominant image with their foundation's charism and enter into a period of revitalization. This process is marked by three features: a transforming response to the signs of the times; a reappropriation of the founding charism; and a profound renewal of the life of prayer, faith, and centeredness in Christ.

In responding to the signs of their times these communities gave to others some claim over themselves. Their renewal was not insular. The founding charism of the community may be

---

11. See Cada, *Shaping the Coming Age,* p. 46.

characterized as its institutional Dream. During each transition period in the life history of the religious order this institutional Dream must be reworked anew into the life of the group. In renewing their life of faith, prayer, and centeredness in Christ, community members deepen the meaning of their life and provide support for one another. During times of transition, then, religious communities also need to examine their commitments. Some change may be called for; at the very least, a significant reworking of these centers of passion and energy will be necessary.

Mary's practice of the virtue of fidelity

The commitment of Mary, the mother of Jesus, offers another illustration of the practice of the virtue of fidelity.[12] Her commitment underwent a considerable evolution during her lifetime. Mary's commitment was schooled by the word of God found in the Old Testament and by the practices of piety and the Law taught and lived by her family and the elders of her community. However, she also learned to listen for God's word in places other than the Scriptures and tradition. Mary pondered in her heart the word of God and of her contemporaries. She also reflected on the events and circumstances of her life.

This dialogue with elements of the internal currents of her life, her Dream, readied Mary for the radical change in her commitment that was her response to the Annunciation. Though Luke tells us she was "deeply disturbed" by the words of the angel, Mary did not become scandalized that the transcendent and so totally Other Yahweh should become so intimate and immanent. At the Annunciation, Mary could not have known what Yahweh's role for her son would be. She practiced fidelity in that she gave prominence to her Dream and, with her "thy will be done to me according to thy word," yielded to Another some claim over her life.

Although Mary continued to live within the tenets of Hebrew Law and the word of God in Scripture, her commitment was

---

12. In his *Should Anyone Say Forever?* Haughey develops a similar example in more detail.

radically transformed. Her life was now a mixture of the old and the new.

It is doubtful that Mary could have been aware of what fidelity would require of her as she witnessed the maturation of her son; church leaders' response to him; his condemnation, death, and resurrection; and Pentecost. Her perception of her son's identity needed to change from offspring to Lord. Faithfulness would not have come easily for Mary, any more than it does for any other man or woman. She could just as well have rejected the spirit of her Dream instead of accepting it and living its uncertainty. Like the rich young man of the gospels, Mary could have remained isolated in her virtue and refused to yield to another any claim over herself.

We have romanticized the life of Mary throughout Church history. She is, however, the image of the Church and of each Christian only because her days were so similar to ours. Mary's life illustrates what fidelity to oneself and to the community can mean in one person's life.

Conclusion

The practice of fidelity is difficult, especially during an age of transition. At times it is even painful. Yet this suffering is no greater than the consequences of betraying one's Dream and remaining isolated from others. To question one's life commitments is a necessary and natural part of adult life, compatible with the virtue of fidelity. When they risk deepening their commitments, men and women need also to accept the possibility that if these promises no longer symbolize the deep directions and currents in their lives, they may have to change their commitments to themselves, to others, and to their God.

Permanent commitments are possible during a transitional age. They are still the best way to grow. To flourish they demand the practice of the virtue of fidelity; that is, they require that individuals struggle with the question of who they are and continually rework their answer as they face the challenges, relationships, and disappointments in their life.

Fidelity to one's Dream and nurturing an ability to allow others to make some claim over one's life demand that people live with passion and vitality; that they struggle with intimacy and share the action and the peril of their age. This task is difficult; its challenge great. To live without fidelity, though, is ultimately to run the risk of being judged as never having lived at all.

Chapter Ten

Bearing the heat of the transition without burning out

In Sister Susan Hennessey's view, her difficulties began with the new pastor's arrival.[1] Like many of her contemporaries in Church ministry, this thirty-eight-year-old parish team member feels the pressures of several parish duties. She helps moderate the youth group, attends parish meetings, visits hospitalized parishioners, coordinates youth and adult religious education, and counsels couples. In addition, Sister Hennessey has responsibilities to her religious community and tries to carve out some leisure time for herself. "I did fine until we got a new pastor last year," she says with an exhausted sigh. "Within two months I had started to burn out." She now takes antacid pills and worries that she may have an ulcer. "He seems to resent my presence and I feel as if he's looking over my shoulder all the time," she says. "He never has a good word to say to anyone. Sometimes the tension at parish staff meetings is so thick you could cut it with a knife."

Quite a different set of problems confronts Father Bill Mahler. Ordained twenty-five years ago, Father Mahler has spent the last ten years in a parish where, except for a part-time youth minister and secretary, he carries all the responsibility for

---

1. All names used in this chapter are fictitious. Any resemblance to persons living or dead is merely coincidental.

parish duties. With the number of "one priest parishes" increasing yearly in his diocese, Father Mahler's situation is not so unusual. "I'm really running dry," he says in a quiet manner. "It's as if I've used up all that I have in this Church. I feel lonely much of the time and often wonder just what I'm doing with my life. More and more, I grow tired of hearing about people's problems and balk at preparing and preaching homilies." Plagued by chronic fatigue, Father Mahler finds it increasingly difficult to make decisions, meet with parishioners, or go to parish council meetings. "When I go home at night," he says, "I'm too tired to move. There's tension around my neck, over my shoulders, and down my arms."

What is happening to these two Church ministers? Though their circumstances are dissimilar, both feel exhausted, depressed, and demoralized. The experience of Sister Hennessey and Father Mahler is one that is increasingly common among religious professionals: both of them are "burning out."

In recent years, interest in the cycle of burnout among priests, sisters, and brothers has grown rapidly. More people are asking: "What is burnout and what are its characteristics and causes?" "Why are some religious professionals afflicted by it while others appear immune?" "Is the risk of developing burnout greater during the present age of transition?" "What can be done about it?" Stated simply, people are wondering if, in fact, burnout is an inevitable part of ministry in today's Church. These questions will be explored in this chapter.

To develop a full understanding of the effects of stress in today's transitional Church and their relationship to the experience of burnout, several areas need to be explored. I will first define burnout and identify and describe its phases. Next, I will look at stress, explore its relationship to physical and mental health, and catalogue those factors that place Church ministers at high risk to burnout. Finally, I will offer practical ways of coping with burnout in both ourselves and others.

What is burnout?

Burnout is a debilitating psychological condition brought about by unrelieved stress in ministry.[2] It leaves people emotionally, physically, and spiritually exhausted. The burned-out sister, brother, or priest experiences four symptoms: little or no energy, a lowered resistance to illness, an increase in pessimism and dissatisfaction, and greater inefficiency in ministry.

In the beginning phases of burnout, Church ministers experience a loss of their health more than the onset of a disease. A lingering cold, for example, that feeling of tiredness that a few days vacation does not seem to relieve, or the experience of working longer hours but accomplishing less and less can all be warning signs that we are slipping into the cycle of burnout. Asked about involvement in ministry ten years from now but under present conditions and with the same people, the burned-out religious professional thinks immediately, "I'd rather be dead!"

Burnout is a progressive condition and occurs over a period of time. It can also reoccur many times during an individual's life. Consider the young religious brother who is a teacher. Early in the life of his ministry, this man's enthusiasm is great and obvious to others. He coaches sports and supervises extracurricular activities in addition to his teaching responsibilities. Unable to say "no," his ministry and students become his entire life. Adult friends and community members are neglected, personal interests ignored, the development of his spiritual life delayed, and renewing leisure activities dropped. Over the course of several months this enthusiastic man begins to change. More irritable than at the outset of his ministry, he often feels overwhelmed and complains that students are ungrateful for his efforts. He misses deadlines at school, flies off the handle in the face of even

2. For additional discussion of the burnout phenomenon, see Jerry Edelwich and Archie Brodsky, *Burnout* (New York: Human Sciences Press, 1980); Ayala M. Pines, Elliot Aronson, and Ditsa Kafry, *Burnout: From Tedium to Personal Growth* (New York: Free Press, 1981); Robert L. Veninga and James P. Spradley, *The Work-Stress Connection: How to Cope with Job Burnout* (Boston: Little, Brown, and Co., 1981). The discussion in this section is adapted from these sources.

minor frustration, and becomes cynical about the school's administrators. Community life is judged to be empty and superficial. Rather than making a change in himself and the way in which he chooses to live his life, this burned-out Church minister asks his provincial for a change in ministry and community. He hopes his new working and living situations will relieve his difficulties. They might for a short time. However, if he fails to reorder his priorities, reestablish his relationships, meet some of his personal and spiritual needs, and give his ministry an important but not exclusive place in his life, he will burn out quickly again.

The stages of burnout

On their journey from enthusiasm and empathy to burnout and apathy, Church ministers appear to pass through five stages.[3] The first is the *honeymoon* stage. During it priests, sisters, and brothers feel enthusiastic and perfectly matched to their ministry. "Honeymooning" religious professionals on their way to burning out may go for months without taking a day off. Their enthusiasm comes, in part, from their strong desire to succeed in ministry and to meet some unconscious needs. People have a number of reasons for becoming involved in Church ministry. Some are easily identified, others are not so obvious. A religious sister, for example, may be involved in social services because of her strong need to help others. However, she might also choose this ministry because of her strong need to be needed by others or because she desires to learn more about herself. Although most people will own up to their desire to help others, those reasons for choosing ministry that are not so laudable are often kept out of awareness.

The many unrealistic expectations that "honeymooners" have for themselves and for those whom they serve also help to explain the enthusiasm so evident during the first stage of burnout.

---

3. Grateful acknowledgment is made to Edelwich and Brodsky, and Veninga and Spradley from whose works this model of burnout is adapted.

An associate pastor may unrealistically expect to be an immediate success in ministry. He will be able to reach those parishioners with whom his colleagues have failed to make any inroads. Failing to see his narcissistic idealism as grandiose and magical, this man believes that his presence will make all the difference in the parish. Other honeymooners in ministry expect to be appreciated by all whom they serve. Still others expect that their training for ministry will prove to be sufficient, that all of those with whom they work will be highly motivated, and that simple solutions will remedy rather complex and difficult problems. Stated simply, the honeymooning Church minister believes in magic. At the heart of all the unrealistic expectations that these people bring to ministry is this idea: by performing certain services for people, they will bring about magical changes in those served and in themselves. Anyone who has experienced this stage of burnout knows only too well that the belief in magic dies hard.

How can people persist in their unrealistic hopes even when these are not confirmed? They do so by judging not that their magical solutions have failed but rather that they have not yet found the right formula. A closer look at honeymooners can throw some light on their reasons for arriving at this conclusion. To begin with, they are overinvested in their ministry. Many will work between twelve and sixteen hours a day seven days a week. They often bring their work home. This cycle of unlimited commitment to ministry gives rise to a problem: the longer people neglect their personal, spiritual, and interpersonal lives, the more they deteriorate. When ministry ceases to furnish the rewards it once did, these men and women are highly vulnerable to burnout.

Furthermore, many Church ministers overidentify with their ministry. Such a situation is detrimental to those being served because the minister's emotional well-being becomes dependent upon his or her clients', students', parishioners', or patients' living up to unrealistic expectations.

Honeymooners, then, are often overcommitted to and overidentified with their ministry. They are also learning two bad habits that set the stage for *fuel depletion*, the second phase of burnout: one, they are not only using up the energy that helps them adapt to stress but they are also failing to replenish that energy; and two, they are not maintaining a balance in their lives between ministry, spiritual and interpersonal life, and realistic personal, leisure, and recreational needs.

A feeling of stagnation and a vague sense of loss are early warning signs that an individual is moving into fuel depletion. The formerly enthusiastic associate pastor, for example, begins to think that it would be nice to have some time for leisure, friends, and a day off or vacation. He becomes increasingly uncomfortable with the small world he has created for himself. Whereas he once had many interests, he finds now that his approach to ministry has led to the atrophy of those interests. Here is the core of the burnout cycle in ministry: the creation of a small world. When religious professionals attempt to meet all their emotional, spiritual, physical, and psychological needs through ministry they are shrinking their world and setting themselves up for burnout.

The stagnation of the fuel depletion stage often begins with the discovery that it is not so easy as anticipated to see, let alone assess, the results of one's labors in ministry. People feel stalled after an initial burst of enthusiasm. They are still doing ministry but it can no longer make up for their unmet personal, interpersonal, and spiritual needs. If these needs remain unfulfilled, priests, sisters, and brothers will not be able to continue in ministry for long. When the pressures of overwork destroy or seriously damage people's personal relationships or interfere with their ability to form any relationships at all, we have a situation that demands some attention. It would be a mistake, however, to describe everyone who burns out as a victim of the demands of ministry. People choose to live in a small world; they are not coerced. Instead, they might make this choice because they are captivated by the allure of ministry, are unaware of the consequences of overinvolvement and overidentification, or lack much of a personal life in the first place.

The choice to do too much in ministry and not enough elsewhere begins sometimes as a desire to escape from an unsatisfactory personal situation or to compensate for other areas in life that are found wanting. A religious woman, for example, may avoid many of the tensions in her community by overinvolving herself in ministry. She argues that she is unable to attend many meals, community prayers, or even the group's meetings because of the demands of her work. Whether or not one's personal, spiritual, or interpersonal life is impoverished prior to overimmersion in ministry, all tend to become so afterward. For the religious man who is a teacher, fuel depletion means that "blue Monday" becomes "blue Tuesday" and "blue Wednesday." During the month of May he wakes up in his southern California community hoping for a "snow holiday."

At some point late in the second stage, many of the most frequent symptoms of burnout in ministry appear. People become increasingly dissatisfied with their work. They are also less efficient than in the past. Decisions are delayed, creativity wanes, and jadedness, cynicism, and accidents increase. Priests, sisters, and brothers who are burning out find an inverse relationship between the time they spend in ministry and the quality of their work. A special kind of inefficiency occurs in ministry when people become callous and indifferent to suffering. Church ministers in fuel depletion often experience insomnia or awake earlier than usual in the morning. They are more fatigued than usual and notice an increase in their escape activities. Smoking, drinking alcohol or beverages that contain caffeine, spending money, or using tranquilizers increases. Failing to attend to their own needs in a healthy manner and lacking a support system, priests, sisters, and brothers in the second stage of burnout find that they are still doing ministry but are also beginning to wonder what ministry is doing to them.

The third and fourth stages of burnout are referred to as *chronic symptoms* and *crisis*. During both of them, people experience a great deal of frustration in their ministry. This frustration can arise suddenly or sink in over a long period of time, leaving Church ministers with a feeling of inner emptiness and doubt about themselves and the efficacy of their work. There are many causes for the frustration. To begin with, about the third stage of burnout people become aware of the gap that exists between the reality of their ministry and their original expectations for it. A young religious teacher, for example, faces the fact that not everyone is motivated to learn. A parish priest realizes that not all of his parishioners are enthusiastic about his projects. The members of a parish team become aware that all of them are not equally cooperative and that this form of ministry is not a panacea.

In addition, during the chronic-symptoms stage of burnout people often feel powerless to change things. Therapists realize that not all clients will change and that they might not be the ones to make a difference in the lives of these men and women. These feelings of powerlessness have a corrosive effect on the self-esteem of Church ministers who have little else in their lives save their ministry.

A number of people also begin to feel defeated, unappreciated, and angry during burnout's third stage. Others engage in self-pity while still others feel they are beating their heads against a wall of indifference. One former teacher described his frustration this way:

> None of us can grow, professionally or otherwise, without positive reinforcement. Try and get some. A teacher is observed twice a year, in the spring and fall, when the superintendent calls in the teacher ratings. The principal, who has little knowledge of the teacher or subject, then comes into the classroom and evaluates things that are irrelevant to the learning process. I was told—and it still angers me—that I did not keep sharp enough pencils on my desk. It didn't matter that I had revised the school's American literature curriculum. It didn't matter that I had started the district's first successful theater program with no funding and no assistance. But let there be a dime jammed into the coke machine after rehearsal, and you can be sure I will be held responsible.[4]

There are three main areas in which burnout's frustration manifests itself: psychosomatic illness; unhealthy indulgence in

---

4. Adapted from Edelwich and Brodsky, *Burnout,* pp. 134-35.

food and in drugs such as caffeine, alcohol, and nicotine; and damage to personal, community, and ministry relationships. Some people, for example, complain of backaches, headaches, and other aches and pains that appear tension related. Others abuse alcohol or greatly increase their daily consumption of coffee. Still others become angry and short-tempered.

The chronic-symptoms stage is the most critical one in the burnout cycle, for what we do with our frustration at this point determines whether or not we will break the cycle or fall deeper into burnout.

People respond to burnout's frustration in three general ways. They use it as a source of destructive energy; they turn it into constructive energy; or they walk away licking their wounds. The first group use the energy created by frustration in a self-destructive way. They engage in a frenzy of activity, trying to deny the frustrating situation, or they attempt to change the unchangeable "givens" of a situation rather than those aspects over which they have some control. For example, a religious sister involved in health-care ministry experiences frustration because her supervisor fails to be as supportive as she would wish. In part, the supervisor's lack of positive affirmation is due to her own rather critical and reserved personality. Instead of seeking her support elsewhere in her life and ministry, the sister in question demands that the supervisor change her behavior. Not surprisingly, such an approach leads only to more frustration. Accepting the givens in a ministry situation does not mean to give up. Instead, it leads people to change what they can and live with what cannot be realistically remedied.

The second group use their frustration as a springboard out of the burnout cycle. They realize that behind their depression and frustration is considerable anger. This emotion is turned outward and into action. Consider the religious brother who feels frustrated with his teaching ministry. He has neglected his friends, cut off his leisure pursuits, allowed his spiritual life to deteriorate, and by making ministry the exclusive center in his life created a small world for himself. Frustrated and angry that he has little time for himself and those aspects of his life that are important to him, he uses his anger to make some changes. This man develops the ability to say "no" to requests that he cannot realistically meet. He struggles to make contact with former friends, finds enjoyment again in leisure pursuits, and puts time aside for retreat, prayer, and the development of his interior life. This man could have used his frustration destructively by hurling himself into even greater activity or by protesting that others should make fewer demands on his time and energies. Instead, he regains some control over his life and begins to set meaningful limits.

Finally, a third group manage the frustration of their chronic-symptoms stage by walking away from ministry. Instead of expressing their frustration, they prefer to lick their wounds. Even here, however, some Church ministers catch themselves walking away from their concern and idealism. They reverse the process by getting angry, asserting themselves and making changes, and returning to ministry in a healthy way.

The fourth or crisis stage of burnout is a critical one. Those Church ministers who reach it become obsessed with their frustrations. They are extremely pessimistic, exhibit serious physical and emotional symptoms, are filled with self-doubt, and develop an escapist mentality. The pastor, for example, who previously delivered better than adequate homilies now seriously questions his ability to say anything of value to his parishioners. For many religious professionals in the crisis stage of burnout, escape from ministry appears to be the only way out.

The fifth and final stage of burnout, characterized by apathy, is called *hitting the wall*. Having started out in ministry caring for others, people in this stage now care mainly about their own survival, health, sanity, and peace of mind. A priest who has "hit the wall," for example, might view his ministry as a "job." He will put in the minimal number of hours but his heart is no longer in the work. He just does not want to be bothered anymore. His indifference is a natural reaction to chronic frustration. Unlike the shallow enthusiasm of the honeymooner, the apathy experienced in the final stage of burnout embeds itself deeply into a person's character. Of all the stages of burnout, this final one is the hardest to bounce back from. Stemming from a decision reached over a period of time to simply stop caring, it is the most settled and deep-seated state. Taking the longest to arrive at, it can last for a lifetime without proper intervention.

In summary, there are five stages in the burnout cycle. Early on, people's symptoms are rarely severe. Even as they move toward burning out priests, sisters, and brothers may experience more a loss of health than the onset of a disease. People who burn out fail to manage stress adequately and feel increasingly isolated. They identify easily with this quip by a burned-out middle-aged pastor: "In Church ministry it's an unwritten policy that you work together but burn out alone." Without appropriate intervention burnout can be extremely hazardous to our physical, emotional, and spiritual health. An understanding of the relationship between stress and burnout will enhance our understanding of the cycle of burnout and start us thinking about ways to intervene.

Burnout and stress

Hard work, long hours, or even insufficient sleep do not necessarily lead to burnout. Church ministers' failure to manage stress appropriately is the real culprit in their burnout story. Stress is caused by any event or circumstance that places an extra demand on people and requires them to adjust.[5] Consider the

---

5. A few of the many excellent sources for information on stress are Bishops' Commission on Priestly Life and Ministry, *The Priest and Stress* (Washington, D.C.: United States Catholic Conference, 1982); James J. Gill, "Burnout: A Growing Threat in Ministry," *Human Development* 1 (Summer 1980): 21-27; Thomas A. Kane and Anna Polcino, *Education Manual for Stress, Affirmation, and Growth Workshop* (unpublished manuscript, 1981); Sehnert, *Stress/Unstresss;* Kristen Wenzel, *Turnover and Burnout among Vocation and Formation Directors: An Exploratory Survey* (Washington, D.C.: Center for Applied Research in the Apostolate, 1982); Robert L. Woolfolk and Frank C. Richardson, *Stress, Sanity, and Survival* (New York: New American Library, 1978).

parish priest whose car breaks down unexpectedly. The time required for its repair forces him to make several changes in his schedule. Some stress events place special demands on a person even though the events were anticipated. The father of a religious brother dies after a long illness. Though anticipated, the death has an impact on this Church minister and gives rise to a myriad of feelings. However, stress results not only from unhappy or unpleasant experiences but also from an outstanding achievement, a promotion at work, ordination, getting married, and many other life changes.

Research has shown that stress, unless controlled, frequently leads to a greater incidence of physical and psychiatric difficulties.[6] People who suffer from chronic stress often report three to four times the normal frequency of emotional and physical illness. On the basis of these findings, one can easily conclude that American society is a stressful one. Just look at the health statistics. About twenty-five million Americans have high blood pressure, one million suffer heart attacks each year, and an estimated eight million men and women have stomach ulcers. Twelve million Americans are said to be alcoholic, and more than two hundred and thirty million prescriptions for tranquilizers are filled each year.[7]

The results of a recent survey also verify that nearly everyone experiences stress in daily living. Forty-one percent of people polled reported a *strong* need to reduce stress in their daily lives. Another 41 percent said they felt *some* need to do so. Only 18 percent felt no need to reduce the amount of stress in their lives.[8]

Changes in family life in America are causing additional stress for a number of people. Nearly half of all marriages contracted

---

6. For a review of the literature linking stress to physical and psychological illness, see Sammon, "Age Thirty Catholic Religious Professional Men," pp. 37-46.

7. See Sehnert, *Stress/Unstress,* p. 14.

8. See General Mills, Inc., *Family Health in an Era of Stress, 1978-79* (Minneapolis: General Mills, Inc., 1979). Copies of this report can be obtained from General Mills Corporate Headquarters, 9200 Wayzata Boulevard, Minneapolis, Minn., 55440.

today will end in divorce, and 40 percent of all children born in this decade will spend part of their growing years in single-parent households. The average American family moves once every seven years, with 20 percent of all families in the country moving each year.[9]

The changing nature of roles within society, dramatic developments in Church ministry, and the many features unique to our present age of transition in the Church and in religious and priestly life also add to the stress experienced by priests, sisters, and brothers.

How does our body respond to these increases in stress? In the face of stress our sympathetic nervous system goes "on alert." The body's metabolism speeds up: heart rate and blood pressure increase, breathing is more rapid, and blood flow to the muscles is greater. In addition, an increased amount of energy is consumed. While under stress, people use a special fuel called "adaptation energy."[10] Its supply is limited and needs to be replenished. Adaptation energy provides the power to mobilize the body and gives us the strength for the fight-or-flight response, which is part of the third phase in most stress reactions. This response takes place as an individual seeks relief from the stress by means of vigorous muscular activity. Finally, as the stress reaction winds down, the body returns to a state of equilibrium.

How does this stress reaction play itself out in actual practice? Consider the following situation. You are driving along a deserted highway on a late August Sunday afternoon. The sun is sinking slowly in the western sky, casting a brilliant orange hue. Returning from lunch with friends, you are feeling quite mellow, the music on the car radio is soothing, your mind is wandering freely, and all appears "right" with your world. All of a sudden, as if out of nowhere, a car almost parallel to yours moves over into your lane. The driver obviously does not see you. You begin to move off the road to avoid an accident. Blasts of your car's horn appear fruitless in getting the other driver's attention. Your

---

9. See Sehnert, *Stress/Unstress*, p. 32.

10. For a discussion of adaptation energy, see Veninga and Spradley, *Work-Stress Connection*, pp. 21-26, 39, 41, 51-53, 71.

hands grip the wheel tightly, your breathing becomes quicker. The stones from the shoulder of the road begin to pelt the underside of your car. Still the other driver appears unaware of your car and the potential for a serious accident. Your body is tense. You are perspiring. You wish you could run the other driver off the road or wake up from the situation as if it were a bad dream. Any remnant of your previously relaxed mood is now history. All of a sudden the driver of the other car spots you and swerves to the left, taking off quickly. You manage to get your car back on the road. After you have given that now distant driver a piece of your mind in the privacy of your car, you notice that your legs feel weak. You have just experienced the four phases of a stress reaction. Getting home, you will want to tell someone about your near accident and find ways to relax and replenish your adaptation energy.

Clouding our dilemma is the fact that some aspects of our stress reaction appear obsolete. We may have a stone age physiological response to space age religious professional problems. In many present-day situations of stress, for example, we are unable to "fight" or "flee." As a consequence, we are left with high levels of muscular tension. This was the complaint of air traffic controllers during their strike in 1981. Attempting to guide aircraft and thus avoid tragic air catastrophes, the controllers suffered from considerable physical tension. Air traffic controllers and Church ministers who refuse to allow themselves leisure and recreation or who lack a variety of stress safety valves deny themselves opportunities to relieve the tension attendant to contemporary stress. In addition to the fact that many modern ministry situations provide little opportunity to discharge built-up tension, there are several other factors that increase one's risk of burnout. It is to these that we now turn.

Risk factors and burnout

Five factors increase most people's chance of burning out.[11] Rarely does just one of these factors lead to burnout; rather, any

11. Again grateful acknowledgment is made to Edelwich and Brodsky, and Veninga and Spradley from whose works this discussion of risk factors is adapted.

combination of them is a powerful trigger for the exhaustion, depression, and demoralization associated with the experience. First of all, our *perception of stress* directly affects the burnout process. Some Church ministers prone to burning out appear to see disaster in every ministry and community or rectory event. We all, for example, can recall "catastrophizers" for whom every schedule change or unexpected appointment is a crisis. The way in which men and women reacted to the 1979 gas crisis is a case in point. Some brought books to read or made new acquaintances as they waited in long gas lines. Others caught up on overdue correspondence or were thankful that the delay gave them some unexpected quiet time to themselves. By contrast, in New York City at least one man was shot, and in California a pregnant woman was struck by another person waiting in line who catastrophized the experience of delay and waiting. Our perception of stress, then, is a major risk factor in burnout. It is also the one over which we have the greatest control and therefore is the one most amenable to change. In the Church's present transitional age some brothers, sisters, and priests have catastrophized recent losses in familiar structures and styles of life. Their failure to place these changes within a transitional framework has added to the stress they experience. By educating themselves in the history of change during previous Church periods, placing the present situation within a transitional context, and using their energies to walk boldly into the second phase of exploration and darkness, Church ministers will alter their perception of stress and be better able to cope with change.

Personal pressures are another factor contributing to the possibility of burnout. The parish priest, for example, who is moved frequently or who is asked to move from a satisfying communal living situation to living alone because of a ministry assignment has an increased risk of burnout. Again, even those events that we welcome as pleasant changes cause their own measure of stress and deplete our adaptation energy.

If you woke up one morning and found that you were living across the river from the Three Mile Island nuclear plant, you would be experiencing another burnout risk factor, that is, an *environmental demand.* Moving from a rural community to an urban one that is in the flight path of the local airport is another example of the type of stressor classified as an environmental pressure. Also, changes such as adjusting to tight living quarters after a move from spacious ones, and beginning missionary work in a new culture can be classified as environmental pressures.

Ministry problems such as understimulation or feeling as though you are not appreciated increase your risk of burning out. A parish priest, for example, might find his work routine and predictable. Or a religious sister who has spent several years working in her community's formation program may begin to feel that no one appreciates her efforts or the toll her work has taken on her.

Finally, an *insufficient number of stress safety valves* will set one up for that demoralized feeling of burnout. If a Church minister has only one stress safety valve to help deal with the pressures of ministry, it will not be long before the early signs of burnout begin to appear. A man who uses alcohol to relax after a long and taxing day but who has little else to help him unwind might find that the one martini he has before dinner becomes two or three in a short time.

We can intervene almost immediately in two of these five areas that increase our risk of burnout. One, we can alter our perception of stress. Two, we can increase the number of safety valves that we have at our disposal. Included among the latter are exercise, prayer and meditation, support from friends, and vacations and a change of activities.

Church ministry, though, presents a special problem with regard to risk factors that increase the chance of burnout.[12] In addition to those already mentioned there are several more that appear to be unique to many priests, sisters, and brothers. To begin with, their work of ministering is never done. Many parish priests, for example, live where they work and thus there are no

---

12. For a more complete discussion of those burnout risk factors unique to Church ministers, see John A. Sanford's *Ministry Burnout* (Ramsey, N.J.: Paulist Press, 1982).

clear lines as to where "work" begins and ends. A number of these men will report with exasperation that unless they leave the rectory on their day off it is not long before they become entangled in the demands of ministry. Priests face a continual onslaught of funerals, weddings, C.C.D. classes to teach, parishioners to visit and counsel, crises, parish censuses, and a variety of administrative duties. For most men and women in Church ministry, then, there are always loose ends. Rarely can they look at a job and feel that it is finished.

Church ministers, furthermore, cannot always tell if their work is having any effect. A business person closes a deal, a construction worker completes the frame of a house, but a man or woman in ministry does not often see the results of his or her efforts. Psychologist John Sanford speculates that the popularity of building programs among many Church ministers is due to their unfulfilled desire to be able to point to something concrete.

Another risk factor increasing their chance of burnout is that men and women in Church ministry are always dealing with the expectations of others. Parishioners expect their priests to be available always. The dinner hour is the best time to reach a religious professional at home. Although calling then might be convenient for the parishioner, it does little to foster community among those gathered around the table. Sisters, brothers, and priests are expected by some to be continuously pleasant and understanding. Others want them to play a particular role, to dress in a special manner, to be set apart, or to be just like everyone else. Church ministers need a healthy sense of their own identity and some self-esteem to deal realistically with others' expectations.

Priests, sisters, and brothers also find that their work is repetitious and that the nature of Church ministry is such that they are dealing almost continuously with people in need. These factors place a great drain on their energies.

Finally, men and women in ministry must often fill a professional role. This "public person" is real but is also only one aspect of the individual. Those sisters, brothers, and priests who do not provide themselves with a personal life but instead live in their professional role all the time are heading for difficulty. In saying this, I am not implying that religious life or priesthood is a profession. Rather, I am reinforcing again the need for a balance between personal, spiritual, interpersonal, leisure, and ministry needs for effective and rewarding Church service.

Suggestions for coping with burnout

People cope with the stages of burnout in a variety of ways.[13] Some deny that the process is taking place, while others hope that rearranging a few externals will guarantee that all will be well. Some interventions for burnout are genuine, others are false.

A false intervention is similar to a medical treatment that gives symptom relief but does little to alter the course of the disease. It is not too helpful, for example, to administer an analgesic and no other medical services to people who have suffered broken limbs in an accident. Several such interventions are important for this discussion: "workshop highs," "legitimate malingering," "denial and false hopes," the "workaholic trap," "scapegoat reactions," and the "guilt trip."

For a number of today's religious professionals the solution to many of life's challenges and problems is to attend a workshop. Although they can be useful learning tools, workshops are not a panacea. For some people, a workshop is like a "fix." They return from it with a momentary good feeling but find quickly that their style of dealing with stress and their vulnerability to the cycle of burnout remain unchanged. Workshops need to be used as they were intended. At the very least, they are like paid vacations. In attending a workshop, one can get useful information and meet others facing similar challenges and difficulties. A workshop, however, cannot substitute for burned-out Church

13. The following sources suggest realistic interventions for burnout in both oneself and others: Edelwich and Brodsky, *Burnout,* pp. 191-247; Herbert Freudenberger and Geraldine Richelson, *Burnout* (New York: Bantam, 1981); Pines, Aronson, and Kafry, *Burnout,* pp. 103-91; Veninga and Spradley, *Work-Stress Connection,* pp. 75-257.

ministers' difficult task of expanding their small world and changing their way of living.

Legitimate malingering is, perhaps, the most insidious of the false interventions for burnout. Its script reads somewhat as follows. A parish priest is exhausted, demoralized, and overwhelmed by his work. Failing to set limits, he is overextended in ministry and has created an exceedingly small world for himself. This man's pastor, noticing his associate's plight, suggests a few days off from parish duties. The burned-out Church minister readily agrees. Upon returning, however, he is again quickly engulfed by the many unrealistic commitments and activities in his life. When he expresses concern about his tiredness and discouragement, others in the parish are perplexed and point out to him that he has just had a few days off. Legitimate malingering encourages brief vacations but does not attack the central core of burnout: the creation of a small world. Those who take a few days off but fail to expand their small world will again quickly become victims of burnout.

Robert Veninga and James Spradley refer to the denial of burnout's symptoms as the "ostrich response."[14] Most people easily understand the image. This large and odd-looking bird buries its head in the sand at the first sign of danger. So does the Church minister who uses the ostrich response to deal with burnout instead of a more realistic intervention. A sister with a variety of psychosomatic complaints, for example, points out that her mother and uncle also reported these maladies. She refuses to look at the lack of leisure time in her life, the absence of any days off or weekends for recreation, and her overextension in ministry. She might also display false hopes by reassuring any concerned listener that when her current ministry projects wind down she will then make some changes in her life. By that time, this woman may have progressed to the last stage of burnout where change is more difficult and lifelong apathy is a real possibility.

The workaholic trap is a favorite false intervention among religious professionals. Unrealistically overextended in ministry,

---

14. See Veninga and Spradley, *Work-Stress Connection,* pp. 126-29.

a brother, priest, or sister takes a few days off to get some perspective on the dilemma. While away, these Church ministers come to the conclusion that they are not really overinvested and overcommitted; rather, they are just not well organized. Upon returning to their ministry they attempt to reorganize and become more efficient. However, if they are indeed overextended these superficial solutions will quickly be found wanting. Although some Church ministers heading toward burnout may look like workaholics, genuine workaholics do not burn out. Rather, those who live and work with them do. Workaholics are men and women whose desire to work long and hard is intrinsic. Their work habits also almost always exceed the prescriptions of their job and the expectations of the people with whom and for whom they work. Some workaholics use their work as a defense against anxiety, but a number of them are relatively content and do not want to work less.

A scapegoat reaction is blaming others for our burnout difficulties. Although all of us use this defense periodically, it is still a false intervention. Imputing evil motives to others will do little to expand our world, help us to set realistic limits, and achieve a balance between the many important areas in our lives.

Finally, the guilt trip false intervention is rooted in the bionic woman and superman complexes that many religious professionals have. Almost all of us, at one time or another in life, have a rescue complex. We should be able to do it all, regardless of the limits of our time, talents, and resources. In continuing to ascribe to this belief, Church ministers begin to feel guilty when they are not able to achieve all that they expect of themselves. Eventually, this guilt handcuffs them. The type of stress that will lead them to burn out, then, will not be dramatic but instead is rooted in unrealistic expectations that they set for themselves.

Several interventions for burnout can decrease Church ministers' risk of falling prey to the cycle. To begin with, they can develop more realistic expectations of themselves, others, and their ministry. These include expecting to be far from perfect and discarding the false ideal of superman and the bionic woman. They must also learn that others will be far from perfect and that they might have to get along with some very difficult people. In addition, Church ministers should expect to be understimulated at times, to receive insufficient rewards for their work, and to have unrealistic demands placed upon them by others.

Priests, sisters, and brothers also need to examine the ways in which they measure success in their ministry. In doing so, they need to make sure they set realistic goals and focus on their successes as well as their failures, on the process of ministry as well as the results. Also, it is important that Church ministers keep a time perspective. They should not, for example, expect results to happen right away. Finally, religious professionals should not always interpret their failures in ministry self-referentially.

Taking responsibility for themselves and their actions is another way for Church ministers to combat burnout. Raising your consciousness about the stress that exists in your ministry can be helpful. One way to do this is to write down all of the things that you complain about in a typical week of ministry. You can also keep a stress-response diary and write down any physiological changes that you note in stressful situations. Listen to your body. Do you, for example, reach for the Bufferin bottle at the same time each day? If so, check out what is happening to you just prior to this ritual. What was your day like? With whom did you interact? What or who were the sources of stress today?

If we are in the cycle of burnout we must also cut back on excessive hours, learn how to change gears, and expand our world. Church ministers who consistently work twelve to sixteen hours a day are, quite simply, working too much. Their preoccupation with work may be a way of avoiding conflict in other areas of their life or be an indication of their lack of a personal life. It is important that each of us finds activities and interests that will remove our attention from the pressures of ministry. It is also important that we put time aside to enjoy these activities fully.

Some Church ministers find it helpful to ease into their day as a way of combating the burnout cycle. Rising half an hour earlier can give people the feeling that they are not beginning the day in response to a starting gun. Warming up slowly to the day is a concrete way of learning to live by the calendar rather than by a stopwatch.

Furthermore, people need to take control of their perceptions of stress by giving up the false myth that something outside of themselves is completely responsible for the stress they feel, and by accepting some of the unchangeable givens in their ministry. For example, there may never be adequate funding to support all of the projects necessary to have the ideal parish.

It can also be helpful to develop a detached view of your ministry periodically. Such an approach can help put it in perspective. Imagine someone else doing your ministry, think of your ministry as a one-act play, or describe it to an outsider. Taking a stress interview can also help us to step outside our situation and examine the many stressors we experience over time.[15]

Finally, break the Type A pattern in ministry.[16] This term is used to describe those individuals whose approach to life and ministry triples their chances of having a heart attack. Such people have a marked tendency to overplan, creating a sense of time urgency. Consider the parish priest who schedules appointments "back-to-back" without even a five-minute break in between. Such a schedule leaves little room for those unexpected but also frequent interruptions that occur throughout the day of any

---

15. A number of stress inventories are in print. A brief self-test for stress levels developed by T.H. Holmes and R.H. Rahe is familiar to many readers. Sehnert reproduces and discusses this measure in his *Stress/Unstress,* pp. 66-70. In Appendix A readers will find a copy of the Religious Life Experience Survey developed in 1982 to assess life change and stress among religious professional men. Completing this measure will give you some indication of the number of change events experienced during the past twelve months and whether or not these were pleasant or unpleasant stressors for you. Norms for this measure are still being developed.

16. Readers interested in completing a brief self-scored measure of Type A personality features are referred to Appendix B. This screening measure is meant to be just that, a screening measure. Interpretation of scores is also included in Appendix B.

Church minister. Type A personalities are also highly competitive. They need to win. In ministry, their project has to be the biggest and the best. Their perfectionistic tendencies make them tough taskmasters, most especially for themselves. In addition, these men and women engage in polyphasic thinking. Stated simply, they often have ten things on their mind at the same time and their actions clearly reflect this. They will interrupt others midsentence, complete thoughts for them, and be one thought ahead of everyone else.

People with a Type A personality have a strong desire to be recognized and considered a success. They suffer from guilt and find it difficult to relax without feeling guilty. Even their social life gets overplanned and hence often becomes a burden. They overextend themselves and are impatient with any delays or interruptions. Although they are often quite successful, some of them do not live long enough to enjoy it.

To break the Type A pattern people have to discontinue their polyphasic thinking and consider one thing at a time. Next, they should practice listening to others without interrupting them. Listening to others and really understanding what they are saying before giving your response is an excellent way to slow down and work against the Type A pattern. Reading books that demand concentration, particularly spiritual reading materials, also defeats the pattern. Although novels, news magazines, detective stories, and such are entertaining, they often do not slow us down and move us inward. Having a retreat space at home is another good roadblock for a Type A personality on the loose. Be it the corner of a room or another area in the house, an uncluttered space for reflection can help us to center ourselves.

Behind all these recommendations is this point: we cannot care deeply about others unless we also care deeply about ourselves. Church ministers who burn out have ceased to care about themselves and hence are unable to care about anyone else. It will, however, take some time for religious professionals to accept this notion about caring for oneself. In the past this concern has often been judged as selfishness. In reality, it is but a healthy respect for oneself.

Conclusion

In the present age of Church transition, priests, sisters, and brothers are experiencing an increased amount of stress. As old Church forms and understandings of religious and priestly life die, Church ministers have to change and adapt. Views of development during the adult years, fidelity, sexuality, and spirituality are also being transformed. Changes in each of these areas bring their own pressures. In the face of all these developments, men and women in contemporary Church ministry are at high risk to burnout. However, burnout is not an inevitable part of the life of an apostle. We all need to guard against a "small world" mentality, develop an understanding of stress, identify the burnout risk factors in our lives, intervene in the cycle of burnout when we notice it in ourselves or in others, and use realistic interventions to cope with it. We also need to admit to ourselves that in Church ministry "human" effort is enough. Paradoxically, the Christian message is much the same, namely, that it is the Lord who builds the house, not just us.

Epilogue

Charles Dickens could well have been describing our current Church era when he wrote the following:

> It was the best of times, it was the worst of times, it was the age of wisdom, it was the age of foolishness, it was the epoch of belief, it was the epoch of incredulity, . . . it was the spring of hope, it was the winter of despair, we had everything before us, we had nothing before us— . . . in short, . . . some of its noisiest authorities insisted on its being received, for good or for evil, in the superlative degree of comparison only.[1]

The transitional nature of our age makes it appear blessed and cursed at the same time. In reality, the crisis of the present Church era provides us with an exciting challenge: the possibility of conversion.

I was educated for a Church and religious life that had died by the time I reached maturity. The notions I learned early in life were meant for another age, a different understanding of the world. Although I respect the past, I do not miss it. Church forms and religious and priestly life-styles of the first half of this century and earlier were developed for a world and Church that no longer exist. While we need to mourn their passing, we cannot return to them. To do so would be to deny growth, grace,

---

1. Charles Dickens, *A Tale of Two Cities* (New York: Harper and Brothers, 1875), p. 7.

and the possibility of a future. The Second Vatican Council caused a huge shift to occur in what was once thought to be a secure and immobile landscape. When it was over, we were all left standing in a different place. The results of this earthquake are the reality we need to addesss. When frightened, we may think about returning to old forms for security and to get things into order. We need to resist this temptation.

I also believe that real renewal has not yet come to the Church, nor to priestly and religious life. This failure has not been due to ill will or lack of effort; rather, the time has not been right. None of us can rush the movement of a transition. It takes time. First, we needed a lengthy period of breakdown, confusion, and death. Next, we will need an even longer period of search and exploration before we can attempt to move toward a new beginning in the Church and a refoundation of religious life.

This second stage of the transition is an important one for the process of renewal. It will challenge us to ask fundamental questions: How can Christianity be made understandable and believable in this age? How can unbelievers be offered access to a faith they find so absurd? How do we begin to educate for a "world" Church? What is the place of pluralism in the Church? How can the People of God assume their task of informed social criticism? How can Church ministers assume the prophetic task of animation? How can we plan the Church's future?[2]

The Church we hoped for with expectation just twenty years ago will be a longer time in coming. The events of the past two decades, though, have been most important. Because of them, the People of God have undertaken the painful task of growing up in many ways. Today, we are faced with the developing possibility of fashioning what many have long hoped for: an adult Christianity.

---

2. These questions, in part, are based upon those raised by Karl Rahner in his "Planning the Church of the Future," pp. 59-62.

Although contemporary priestly and religious life is dying in many ways, there are also signs of life. A number of priests and men and women religious are developing simplicity in their lifestyle. Others struggle for genuine belief in the face of great uncertainty. Still others are realizing that their ministry is not so much to staff institutions as to take up the prophetic task of animation. Religious and priestly life needs to be on the way to "refounding" itself in ways suitable for a Church struggling to be transformed.

The present Church era has also given Church ministers new opportunities to grow personally, interpersonally, and spiritually. This situation frightens a number of them; their task appears too formidable. Some are wary of intimate relationships, for example, having for so long been warned against particular friendships. Others desire close, warm, and loving relationships but wonder if they have the capacity for them or the skills to make them a possibility. Again, it is important to remember that the process of transition takes time and has a characteristic shape. First, there is the death of old understandings and forms. This stage is followed by a period during which more mistakes may be made than successes realized. Only then can there be a new beginning. Although the process of growth is never easy, its rewards are great.

Today, as religious professionals, we are growing ever more aware of our own development over the course of the life cycle. As part of our efforts, we need to examine during every period of transition our understandings of commitments, vows of poverty, chastity, and obedience, and faith and spirituality. This normal and necessary task of adulthood gives us the opportunity to enrich and deepen our understanding of what is most essential and important in life. At the heart of our development as adults and that of Christian spirituality is this question: "Where does your treasure lie?" It is in formulating our answer that we open up the possibility of coming to know ourselves, others, and God.

We needed the current transition in the Church and in religious and priestly life. It has roused us from our sleep and challenged us to look at what or to whom we have given our hearts. As Christians, the transition is a part of our call to discipleship and the Paschal Mystery. Although there has been some loss and pain, there is also the possibility of transformation. In the midst of our present transition, and during any other, we do well to remember that "in every winter's heart there is a quivering spring."[3] As we search for it, we need to rely on faith to guide us, hope to sustain us, and love to support us on our journey.

3.Credited to Kahlil Gibran, *The Wisdom of Gibran* (Philosophical Library) in "Quotable Quotes," *Reader's Digest,* March 1983.

Appendix A

RELIGIOUS LIFE EXPERIENCE SURVEY

Copyright 1982 — Sean D. Sammon

Listed below are a number of events which sometimes bring about change in the lives of those who experience them and which necessitate social readjustment. *Please check those events which you have experienced in the recent past and indicate the time period during which you have experienced each event.* Be sure that all check marks are directly across from the item to which they correspond.

Also for each item checked, *please indicate the extent to which you viewed the event as having either a positive or negative impact on your life at the time the event occurred.* That is, indicate the type and extent of impact that the event had. A rating of − 3 would indicate an extremely negative impact. A rating of 0 suggests no impact either positive or negative. A rating of + 3 would indicate an extremely positive impact.

	0 to 6 mo	7 mo to 1 yr	extremely negative	moderately negative	somewhat negative	no impact	slightly positive	moderately positive	extremely positive
1. Death of a close family member:									
a. mother	___	___	− 3	− 2	− 1	0	+ 1	+ 2	+ 3
b. father	___	___	− 3	− 2	− 1	0	+ 1	+ 2	+ 3
c. brother	___	___	− 3	− 2	− 1	0	+ 1	+ 2	+ 3
d. sister	___	___	− 3	− 2	− 1	0	+ 1	+ 2	+ 3
e. grandmother	___	___	− 3	− 2	− 1	0	+ 1	+ 2	+ 3
f. grandfather	___	___	− 3	− 2	− 1	0	+ 1	+ 2	+ 3
g. other (specify) _____	___	___	− 3	− 2	− 1	0	+ 1	+ 2	+ 3
2. Commencing a love relationship	___	___	− 3	− 2	− 1	0	+ 1	+ 2	+ 3

3. Major change in eating habits (much more or much less food intake) _____ −3 −2 −1 0 +1 +2 +3

4. Major change in relationship with parents _____ −3 −2 −1 0 +1 +2 +3

5. Death of a close friend _____ −3 −2 −1 0 +1 +2 +3

6. A lot more or a lot less association with other community members due to work commitments _____ −3 −2 −1 0 +1 +2 +3

7. Outstanding personal achievement _____ −3 −2 −1 0 +1 +2 +3

8. A lot more or a lot less trouble with your religious superiors _____ −3 −2 −1 0 +1 +2 +3

9. Changed work situation (different work responsibility, major change in working conditions, working hours, etc.) _____ −3 −2 −1 0 +1 +2 +3

10. Gaining new community member(s) _____ −3 −2 −1 0 +1 +2 +3

11. Appointment to a new position within your religious order or congregation _____ −3 −2 −1 0 +1 +2 +3

12. Serious illness or injury of close family member:

    a. father _____ −3 −2 −1 0 +1 +2 +3
    b. mother _____ −3 −2 −1 0 +1 +2 +3
    c. sister _____ −3 −2 −1 0 +1 +2 +3
    d. brother _____ −3 −2 −1 0 +1 +2 +3
    e. grandfather _____ −3 −2 −1 0 +1 +2 +3
    f. grandmother _____ −3 −2 −1 0 +1 +2 +3
    g. other (specify) _____ −3 −2 −1 0 +1 +2 +3

233

	0 to 6 mo	7 mo to 1 yr	extremely negative	moderately negative	somewhat negative	no impact	slightly positive	moderately positive	extremely positive
13. Terminating a love relationship	___	___	−3	−2	−1	0	+1	+2	+3
14. Sexual difficulties	___	___	−3	−2	−1	0	+1	+2	+3
15. Major change in number of arguments with other community members (a lot more or a lot fewer arguments)	___	___	−3	−2	−1	0	+1	+2	+3
16. Moving to a new apostolic work situation without changing the type of work that you are doing	___	___	−3	−2	−1	0	+1	+2	+3
17. Major change in sleeping habits (much more or much less sleep)	___	___	−3	−2	−1	0	+1	+2	+3
18. Major change in type of ministry	___	___	−3	−2	−1	0	+1	+2	+3
19. Major change in living conditions of your local community	___	___	−3	−2	−1	0	+1	+2	+3
20. Close friend moving from your community to another	___	___	−3	−2	−1	0	+1	+2	+3
21. Trouble with employer (in danger of losing job, being suspended, demoted, etc.)	___	___	−3	−2	−1	0	+1	+2	+3
22. Change in local administration connected with your ministry	___	___	−3	−2	−1	0	+1	+2	+3
23. Ordination	___	___	−3	−2	−1	0	+1	+2	+3
24. Change in local religious superiors	___	___	−3	−2	−1	0	+1	+2	+3
25. Major change in personal habits (dress, manners, associations, etc.)	___	___	−3	−2	−1	0	+1	+2	+3

#	Item		-3	-2	-1	0	+1	+2	+3
26.	Thoughts of leaving religious life	——	-3	-2	-1	0	+1	+2	+3
27.	Final profession	——	-3	-2	-1	0	+1	+2	+3
28.	Major change in closeness of family members (increased or decreased closeness)	——	-3	-2	-1	0	+1	+2	+3
29.	Commencing psychotherapy	——	-3	-2	-1	0	+1	+2	+3
30.	Major change in use of alcohol (increased or decreased use)	——	-3	-2	-1	0	+1	+2	+3
31.	A friend leaving religious life	——	-3	-2	-1	0	+1	+2	+3
32.	Change of residence	——	-3	-2	-1	0	+1	+2	+3
33.	Being fired from a job	——	-3	-2	-1	0	+1	+2	+3
34.	Major change in understanding of religious vows and the practical living out of them:								
	a. poverty	——	-3	-2	-1	0	+1	+2	+3
	b. chastity	——	-3	-2	-1	0	+1	+2	+3
	c. obedience	——	-3	-2	-1	0	+1	+2	+3
	d. special community vow (specify) _____	——	-3	-2	-1	0	+1	+2	+3
35.	Financial problems concerning school (in danger of not having sufficient money to continue)	——	-3	-2	-1	0	+1	+2	+3
36.	Failing a course	——	-3	-2	-1	0	+1	+2	+3
37.	Terminating psychotherapy	——	-3	-2	-1	0	+1	+2	+3
38.	Taking a leave of absence from your religious order or congregation	——	-3	-2	-1	0	+1	+2	+3
39.	Major personal injury or illness	——	-3	-2	-1	0	+1	+2	+3
40.	Major change in use of nonprescribed medications (increased or decreased use)	——	-3	-2	-1	0	+1	+2	+3

#	Item	0 to 6 mo	7 mo to 1 yr	extremely negative	moderately negative	somewhat negative	no impact	slightly positive	moderately positive	extremely positive
41.	Decision to postpone ordination	___	___	-3	-2	-1	0	+1	+2	+3
42.	Major change in domestic responsibilities (increased or decreased involvement in cooking, cleaning, etc.)	___	___	-3	-2	-1	0	+1	+2	+3
43.	Beginning apostolic work for the first time	___	___	-3	-2	-1	0	+1	+2	+3
44.	Beginning a new school experience at a higher academic level (graduate school, professional school)	___	___	-3	-2	-1	0	+1	+2	+3
45.	Failing an important exam	___	___	-3	-2	-1	0	+1	+2	+3
46.	Living with an order or congregation other than the one to which you belong	___	___	-3	-2	-1	0	+1	+2	+3
47.	Major change in religious practices	___	___	-3	-2	-1	0	+1	+2	+3
48.	Move to living alone	___	___	-3	-2	-1	0	+1	+2	+3
49.	Dropping a course	___	___	-3	-2	-1	0	+1	+2	+3
50.	Changing a major	___	___	-3	-2	-1	0	+1	+2	+3
51.	Major change in use of prescribed medications									
52.	A change in provincial government	___	___	-3	-2	-1	0	+1	+2	+3
53.	Retreat experience	___	___	-3	-2	-1	0	+1	+2	+3
54.	Decision to postpone final vows	___	___	-3	-2	-1	0	+1	+2	+3
55.	Ending of formal schooling	___	___	-3	-2	-1	0	+1	+2	+3

56. Joining a religious support group (e.g., cursillo, charismatic group)	___	−3	−2	−1	0	+1	+2	+3
57. Moving to a new local community	___	−3	−2	−1	0	+1	+2	+3
58. Ministry in a situation outside of those institutions operated by your order or congregation	___	−3	−2	−1	0	+1	+2	+3
59. Serious doubt about religious faith ("crisis of faith")	___	−3	−2	−1	0	+1	+2	+3
60. Major change in social activities: e.g., parties, movies, visiting (increased or decreased participation)	___	−3	−2	−1	0	+1	+2	+3
Other recent experiences which have had an impact on your life. List and rate.								
61. _____	___	−3	−2	−1	0	+1	+2	+3
62. _____	___	−3	−2	−1	0	+1	+2	+3
63. _____	___	−3	−2	−1	0	+1	+2	+3

237

Appendix B

SELF-TEST FOR "TYPE A" PERSONALITY

As you can see, each scale below is composed of a pair of adjectives or phrases separated by a series of horizontal lines. Each pair has been chosen to represent two kinds of contrasting behavior. Each of us belongs somewhere along the line between the two extremes. Since most of us are neither the most competitive nor the least competitive person we know, put a check mark where you think you belong between the two extremes.

	1	2	3	4	5	6	7	
1. Doesn't mind leaving things temporarily unfinished	—	—	—	—	—	—	—	Must get things finished once started
2. Calm and unhurried about appointments	—	—	—	—	—	—	—	Never late for appointments
3. Not competitive	—	—	—	—	—	—	—	Highly competitive
4. Listens well, lets others finish speaking	—	—	—	—	—	—	—	Anticipates others in conversation (nods, interrupts, finishes sentences for the other)
5. Never in a hurry, even when pressured	—	—	—	—	—	—	—	Always in a hurry
6. Able to wait calmly	—	—	—	—	—	—	—	Uneasy when waiting
7. Easygoing	—	—	—	—	—	—	—	Always going full speed ahead
8. Takes one thing at a time	—	—	—	—	—	—	—	Tries to do more than one thing at a time, thinks about what to do next

9. Slow and deliberate in speech — — — — — — — Vigorous and forceful in speech (uses a lot of gestures)

10. Concerned with satisfying self, not others — — — — — — — Wants recognition by others for a job well done

11. Slow doing things — — — — — — — Fast doing things (eating, walking, etc.)

12. Easygoing — — — — — — — Hard driving

13. Expresses feelings openly — — — — — — — Holds feelings in

14. Has a large number of interests — — — — — — — Few interests outside work

15. Satisfied with job — — — — — — — Ambitious, wants quick advancement on job

16. Never sets own deadlines — — — — — — — Often sets own deadlines

17. Feels limited responsibility — — — — — — — Always feels responsible

18. Never judges things in terms of numbers — — — — — — — Often judges performance in terms of numbers (how many, how much)

19. Casual about work — — — — — — — Takes work very seriously (works weekends, brings work home)

20. Not very precise — — — — — — — Very precise (careful about detail)

SCORING: Assign a value from 1 to 7 for each score. Total them up. (Turn to the next page for analysis of your score.)

Based on research by Dr. Howard I. Glazer. Reprinted by permission from *Stress/Unstress* by Keith W. Sehnert, M.D., copyright 1981 Augsburg Publishing House.

239

ANALYSIS OF YOUR SCORE

Total score = 110-140: Type A_1.

If you are in this category, and especially if you are over 40 and smoke, you are likely to have a high risk of developing cardiac illness.

Total score = 80-109: Type A_2.

You are in the direction of being cardiac prone, but your risk is not so high as the A_1. You should, nevertheless, pay careful attention to the advice given to all Type A's.

Total score = 60-79: Type AB.

You are an admixture of A and B patterns. This is a healthier pattern than either A_1 or A_2, but you have the potential for slipping into A behavior and you should recognize this.

Total score = 30-59: Type B_2.

Your behavior is on the less-cardiac-prone end of the spectrum. You are generally relaxed and cope adequately with stress.

Total score = 0-29: Type B_1.

You tend to the extreme of non-cardiac traits. Your behavior expresses few of the reactions associated with cardiac disease.

This test will give you some idea of where you stand in the discussion of Type A behavior. The higher your score, the more cardiac prone you tend to be. Remember, though, even B persons occasionally slip into A behavior, and any of these patterns can change over time.